This book is dedicated to
Karen's mother Betty B. Lourie
and Christine's father Stanley A. Baker
for their love and support
and all that they have done for us.

CONTENTS

Introduction vi

UNIT 1 TRAVEL TALK   1
1. The Company of the Sea 4
2. Madrid Memories 8
3. Flying High, but Feeling Low 18
Tying It All Together 23

UNIT 2 ATTITUDES ABOUT ANIMALS   29
1. All for the Love of Fritz 31
2. Can Animals Think? 39
3. Anti-Fur Groups Renew Fur Debate 45
Tying It All Together 49

UNIT 3 FACING CHALLENGES   57
1. 86-Year-Old Man in Marathon for 63rd Time 59
2. Disabled People Find Challenge on the Slopes 63
3. Sounds of Bali 67
4. "Dreams" by Langston Hughes 71
Tying It All Together 73

UNIT 4 BRAINPOWER   79
1. Do You Know Your Right Brain from Your Left? 81
2. Albert Einstein: The Man and the Legends about Him .. 86
3. How Good Is Your Memory? 92
Tying It All Together 96

UNIT 5 CLIMATE CONTROL   103
1. Winter Blues, Summer Blahs 105
2. Climate: A Powerful Force 109
3. What's the Weather? 117
Tying It All Together 124

UNIT 6 FOOD FOR THOUGHT   **129**

1. Finding the Recipe for Success........................132
2. Genetically Altered Tomato Approved................136
3. Red Hot, or Not?.....................................140
4. Plant Power 145
Tying It All Together.................................149

UNIT 7 COMPANIES WITH A CONSCIENCE   **155**

1. Profits with Principles...............................157
2. The Scoop on Ben & Jerry's 162
3. Warm and Fuzzy Soda Bottles 167
Tying It All Together.................................179

UNIT 8 TUNE IN TO TV   **185**

1. The Early Days and Beyond.........................187
2. Can You Imagine a World without It?................192
3. Commercial-Free TV 196
Tying It All Together.................................203

Answer Key 209

INTRODUCTION

For Your Information 1 is a book of high-interest readings, most of which are authentic, for high-beginning or low-intermediate students of English as a second language (ESL). It focuses on the very real needs of students at this level for vocabulary expansion and reading skill-building. It is designed for use in ESL adult-education programs, universities, language institutes, and secondary schools both in the United States and abroad.

For Your Information 1 is made up of eight thematically based units, each of which contains a selection of three or four readings. It is based on the premise that ESL students are able to read at a higher level of English than they can produce. Vocabulary-building and skill-building activities accompany each reading.

An important goal of *For Your Information 1* is to help students become confident readers by increasing their vocabulary base and improving their word-attack skills. It engages them in the process of reading thoughtfully and encourages them to move beyond passive reading. Although it is a reading text, students practice their speaking, listening, and writing throughout *For Your Information 1*. The tasks are varied, accessible, and engaging and they provide stimuli for frequent interaction.

The basic format for each unit in *For Your Information 1* is as follows:

- **Points to Ponder**
  These prereading questions serve to introduce the topic of the unit and get students thinking about that topic.

- **Reading Selections and Accompanying Tasks**
  Each unit contains three or four reading selections on topics of high interest and universal appeal. One of the readings in each unit is an interview with an individual knowledgeable on some aspect of the general topic of that unit. Selections are followed by a combination of comprehension questions and activities to practice new vocabulary and vocabulary in context as well as scanning, skimming, predicting, and separating main from supporting ideas.

INTRODUCTION

- **Tying It All Together**
  Each unit concludes with discussion questions designed to encourage students to think about, distill, and discuss the information they have read about throughout the unit. Following the questions are an interactive vocabulary review and self-test and an activity that is "Just for Fun." The units close with a "Reader's Journal," a place for students to reflect, in writing, on the readings in each unit.

We hope that you and your students enjoy the readings and activities in this text and find them interesting *for your information.*

KLB, CBR

ACKNOWLEDGMENTS

We acknowledge with gratitude the many family members and friends whose seemingly tireless reading, writing, and researching added so much to this book.

Our thanks go also to Adèle Camus of George Mason University, Laura Le Dréan of the University of Houston, Lynn Meng of Union County College, New Jersey, Joe Ryan of Los Angeles City College, and Mehmet Aksu of Drexel University for their discerning suggestions.

Finally, we thank the individuals who so graciously submitted themselves to our interviews, and our editor, Allen Ascher, for his enthusiasm and peerless attention to the details.

TRAVEL TALK

Unit·1

Selections

1. The Company of the Sea .4

2. Madrid Memories 8

3. Flying High, but Feeling Low 18

People travel for many different reasons. Some people travel to visit friends or family. Other people travel for business or education. Still others travel for excitement and adventure. This unit has several articles about travel experiences. Before you read these articles, think about your own feelings about traveling.

POINTS TO PONDER

Answer each of the following questions about yourself. Then discuss your answers in small groups.

1. What do you like most about traveling? Make a list.

   _____
   _____
   _____
   _____

TRAVEL TALK / **UNIT 1**

2. What do you like least about traveling? Make a list.

   _____

   _____

   _____

   _____

3. Which of the following types of vacations appeal to you? Put a 1 in front of your first choice, a 2 in front of your second choice, and so on.

   _____ ski trip   _____ city sightseeing

   _____ tropical island   _____ camping

   _____ cruise   _____ visiting family or friends

   _____ safari   _____ other: _____

4. How important is each of the following factors to you when you choose a vacation destination? Rank them in order of importance.

   _____ weather   _____ a golf course

   _____ scenery   _____ location

   _____ friendly people   _____ interesting sights

   _____ food   _____ tourist facilities

   _____ cost   _____ accommodations

   _____ shopping   _____ other: _____

5. Which factors would make your vacation less enjoyable? Put them in order. Start with the one most likely to ruin your trip.

   _____ bad weather   _____ getting sunburned

   _____ losing your wallet   _____ bad food

   _____ getting sick   _____ poor accommodations

   _____ jet lag   _____ losing your luggage

   _____ bad flight   _____ other: _____

SELECTION 1

The Company of the Sea is an interview with a man who has sailed around the world. This man, Eralp Akkoyunlu, was born in Istanbul, Turkey in 1933. He spent his childhood in Istanbul on an island called Buyukada, which means "big island" in English. Like many of the children on the island, he loved the water, the fish, and the small boats. Sometimes he would go out with fishermen in their boats. Eralp was never afraid of the water.

Eralp's dream was to build a boat and sail it around the world. Lots of people dream of boats. Many people buy boats. Some people build boats, but very few people build their own boat and sail it around the world alone. This is an interview with someone who did.

BEFORE YOU READ

PREREADING DISCUSSION

1. Have you ever been on a sailboat or taken a cruise somewhere? If you have, describe your experience to your classmates.

2. Do you like the feeling of being on a boat? How does it make you feel? Relaxed? Anxious? Excited? Free? Afraid? Helpless? Strong?

3. Sailing on the sea is a popular theme. There are many movies, books, paintings, songs, and poems about life on the sea. Have you seen, read, or heard any of these? Discuss some of your favorite ones with your classmates.

TRAVEL TALK / **UNIT 1**

The Company of the Sea

Tell us a little about yourself and what made you decide to build a boat and sail it around the world.

1   I finished my early education in Turkey and moved to New York for graduate school in computer science at Columbia University. After I finished my Ph.D., I began teaching graduate students at Stonybrook University in New York and then at Brooklyn College. I loved New York and felt like a true New Yorker, but I often missed the sea. One day on vacation in southern Turkey, I realized that what I really wanted to do was build a sailboat and sail around the world. When I returned to New York, I started to work on it.

How long did it take to build the boat? How big is it?

2   I worked full-time at my teaching job during the week and began to build the boat at night and on weekends. It was a long and difficult job. It took me about five years. The boat is thirty-eight feet long. I decided to name the boat *Yosun*, which means "seaweed" in Turkish.

Describe the trip you took on your boat.

3   Because of my job, I was only able to sail during summer vacations, so the trip around the world had to be broken up into small pieces. The first section was from New York to Bermuda. From there, I went to Venezuela, then to the Galápagos Islands and Tahiti. I wandered all through the South Pacific, stopping for long visits to Fiji. Occasionally, I would be joined by friends. But most of the time, my only companions were dolphins and flying fish. Sometimes a bird would stop by to hitchhike or for a little rest. I love the company of the sea and most of all, I love my boat. *Yosun* sails beautifully and is a joy to see.

What are you doing now? Are you planning another trip?

4   Now I divide my time between life on the sea and life in the city. *Yosun* is in southern Turkey, being readied for a second major trip—crossing the Atlantic and then returning to the South Pacific.

SELECTION 1

HOW WELL DID YOU READ?

Read the following statements. If a statement is true, write *T* on the line. If it is false, write *F*.

_____ 1. As a child, Eralp was afraid of the water.

_____ 2. Eralp grew up in Turkey.

_____ 3. *Yosun* was built in Turkey.

_____ 4. Eralp usually sailed alone.

_____ 5. Many people build their own boats and sail around the world.

BUILDING READING SKILLS
ORGANIZING INFORMATION

Here is a list of some important events in Eralp's life. Put them in the correct time order by numbering them from 1 to 8.

_____ went to graduate school at Columbia University

_____ spent his childhood on an island called Buyukada

_____ sailed to Venezuela, the Galápagos Islands, and Tahiti

_____ completed his early education in Turkey

_____ spent five years building *Yosun*

_____ began teaching graduate students

_____ sailed from New York to Bermuda

_____ realized he wanted to build a sailboat and sail it around the world

BUILDING READING SKILLS
LOCATING INFORMATION

Look through the interview for the answers to the following questions. When you find the place in the text that answers the question, underline it. Then write the number of the paragraph in the space provided. Work as quickly as you can.

1. How long did it take Eralp to build his sailboat? (¶ _____)

2. How long is the boat? (¶ _____)

3. What does *Yosun* mean in English? (¶ _____)

4. Where is *Yosun* now? (¶ _____)

5. At what university did Eralp get his Ph.D.? (¶ _____)

TALK IT OVER

DISCUSSION

1. What was Eralp's dream?
2. Why did it take him so long to build his sailboat?
3. Why was his first trip around the world broken up into pieces?
4. What kind of challenges do you think Eralp faced during his journey?

EXPANDING VOCABULARY

Circle the letter of the word or phrase that is closest in meaning to the underlined word.

1. *I loved New York and felt like a <u>true</u> New Yorker, but I often <u>missed</u> the sea.*

   true:
   a. real
   b. lonely
   c. foreign

   missed:
   a. felt bored with
   b. felt the loss of
   c. felt afraid of

2. *I worked full-time at my teaching job during the week and began to build the boat at night and on <u>weekends</u>.*

   a. in the evening
   b. on vacations
   c. on Saturdays and Sundays

3. *The first <u>section</u> was from New York to Bermuda.*

   a. problem
   b. part
   c. job

4. *I <u>wandered</u> all through the South Pacific, stopping for long visits to Fiji.*

   a. traveled without a specific destination
   b. sailed quickly
   c. had many mechanical problems

5. *<u>Occasionally</u>, I would be joined by friends. But most of the time, my only <u>companions</u> were dolphins and flying fish.*

   occasionally:
   a. most of the time
   b. once in a while
   c. luckily

   companions:
   a. company; friends
   b. enemies
   c. animals

France is the country that receives the largest number of tourists worldwide.

SELECTION 2

Madrid Memories is taken from the travel journal of Nancy Stetser, a young woman who was traveling in Spain. This entry describes her thoughts about the first day of her trip.

BEFORE YOU READ

PREREADING DISCUSSION

1. Do you ever keep a journal when you travel? If so, what kinds of things do you record?

2. Do you like to take pictures when you travel? Do you collect souvenirs from the places you visit? If so, what kind?

Madrid Memories

June 23, Madrid

Dear Journal,

1. I like to have new experiences when I travel, but yesterday was too much. It was a day I'll never forget.

2. My plane to Madrid was five hours late. And bumpy. The flight attendant spilled soda on my dress. What a mess! The taxi driver couldn't understand my Spanish. He took me to the wrong hotel, and then he overcharged me.

3. When I got to the right hotel and checked in, I thought my problems were over. I couldn't wait to change out of my stained traveling clothes. But my happiness disappeared as soon as I opened my suitcase. The clothes inside were not mine. They belonged to someone else who had a suitcase that looked just like mine. It was obvious as soon as I opened the suitcase. On top of the carefully folded clothes was the most beautiful silk shawl that I have ever seen in my life.

4. What could I do? I was hungry, tired, angry, and frustrated. I wanted to get some dinner and then go to sleep. It was chilly outside, and I had on only a summer dress. How could I go to dinner in a dirty dress? My eyes went to the open suitcase on the bed. Would anyone mind if I borrowed the gorgeous shawl? I could just borrow it for tonight, I thought, to keep warm and cover the stains. I would be very careful of it and put it back in the suitcase before I contacted the airline in the morning. It sounded like such a good plan. Who would know? Who would care?

5. I put on the shawl and went to look for a place to eat. I wanted to try some of the local food. My friend had given me the names and addresses of a few places. Unfortunately they were all very crowded. Finally, I decided to eat in the hotel restaurant. It was cool outside, but like everything else yesterday, it was my bad luck that the hotel restaurant was very warm. Naturally, I took the shawl off and put it carefully on the back of my chair. I ate my dinner, paid the bill, and left the restaurant. I never thought of the shawl again until I was lying in bed.

6. By then it was too late to call. The restaurant had closed. I could not sleep at all. I was so worried about the shawl. What if someone had taken it? The more I worried, the more nervous I became. At some point I began to have nightmares about going to jail.

7. Fortunately for me, today is a new day. I guess I did sleep a little last night because when I opened my eyes this morning I saw that the red message light on my phone was flashing. I called the front desk, and guess what?! One of the waiters had brought the shawl to the front desk. He had my name and room number from the restaurant bill.

8. I think that this is what traveling is all about: going home with a great story to tell. Especially if it has a happy ending.

SELECTION 2

HOW WELL DID YOU READ?

Read the following statements. If a statement is true, write *T* on the line. If it is false, write *F*.

_____ 1. Nancy likes new experiences.

_____ 2. Her trip to Madrid went well.

_____ 3. She realized immediately that the suitcase in her hotel room wasn't hers.

_____ 4. The weather in Madrid was hot.

_____ 5. Nancy decided not to return the shawl.

_____ 6. She wanted to eat in the hotel restaurant.

_____ 7. The restaurant was very warm.

_____ 8. Nancy purposely left the shawl in the restaurant.

_____ 9. She fell asleep quickly on her first night in Madrid.

_____ 10. The shawl was returned the next day and the story had a happy ending.

BUILDING READING SKILLS

REMEMBERING INFORMATION

Make a list of all the problems that Nancy had during her trip to Madrid.

_____

_____

_____

_____

_____

_____

BUILDING READING SKILLS

LOCATING REASONS

With a partner, look back at Nancy's journal to find the answers to the following questions.

1. Why did Nancy borrow the shawl?

_____

_____

TRAVEL TALK / **UNIT 1**

2. Why did she think the suitcase was hers?

   _____

   _____

3. Why did she eat in the hotel restaurant?

   _____

   _____

4. Why couldn't she sleep well her first night in Madrid?

   _____

   _____

5. Why was the shawl returned to her in the morning?

   _____

   _____

TALK IT OVER

DISCUSSION

1. Have you ever lost your luggage while you were traveling? What happened? How did you handle the situation?

2. Why do you think Nancy decided to wait until morning to call the airline? Why do you think she didn't do it immediately?

3. How do you feel about Nancy's borrowing and wearing the shawl without permission? How would you have behaved in this situation?

4. What is your impression of Nancy? What kind of person do you think she is? How would you describe her?

5. In the last paragraph, Nancy writes, "I think that this is what traveling is all about: going home with a great story to tell." Do you agree with her? What is traveling all about for you?

SELECTION 2

EXPANDING VOCABULARY

A. Circle the letter of the word or phrase that best completes each sentence.

1. Nancy likes to have new _____ when she travels.
   a. problems
   b. happiness
   c. experiences

2. The _____ spilled soda on her dress.
   a. flight attendant
   b. hotel clerk
   c. waiter

3. When Nancy opened the suitcase, she _____ that the clothes belonged to someone else.
   a. worried
   b. realized
   c. borrowed

4. She decided to wear the shawl because it was _____ outside.
   a. warm
   b. stained
   c. chilly

5. That night she was very _____ about the shawl.
   a. angry
   b. worried
   c. hungry

People tend to spend six times more money when they visit a new country than they spend when they travel in their own countries.

B. Circle the letter of the word or phrase that is closest in meaning to the underlined word.

1. *He took me to the wrong hotel, and then he <u>overcharged</u> me.*
   a. charged too much
   b. charged too little
   c. charged the exact amount

2. It was <u>chilly</u> outside, and I had on only a summer dress.

   a. hot
   b. cool
   c. raining

3. Would anyone mind if I borrowed the <u>gorgeous</u> shawl?

   a. silk
   b. big
   c. beautiful

4. I would be very careful of it and put it back in the suitcase before I <u>contacted</u> the airline in the morning.

   a. called
   b. borrowed
   c. worried

5. <u>Fortunately</u> for me, today is a new day.

   a. especially
   b. luckily
   c. definitely

BUILDING VOCABULARY SKILLS
SYNONYMS AND ANTONYMS

Synonyms are words that have similar meanings. For example, *big* and *large* are synonyms because they mean almost the same thing. Antonyms are words that have opposite meanings. For example, *big* and *little* are antonyms because their meanings are opposite to each other. Understanding the relationships between words can help you build your vocabulary and make you a better reader.

Decide if the following pairs of words are synonyms or antonyms. If they are synonyms, circle *S*. If they are antonyms, circle *A*.

1. chilly	cool	S	A
2. bumpy	smooth	S	A
3. gorgeous	beautiful	S	A
4. ordinary	unusual	S	A
5. fortunately	luckily	S	A

SELECTION 2

USE YOUR IMAGINATION

Imagine a different ending to the story. What might have happened if the shawl hadn't been returned? In small groups, make up a new ending. Choose one member of your group to tell the new ending of the story to the rest of the class.

APPLICATION OF INFORMATION

Examine the following travel brochures for vacation trips.

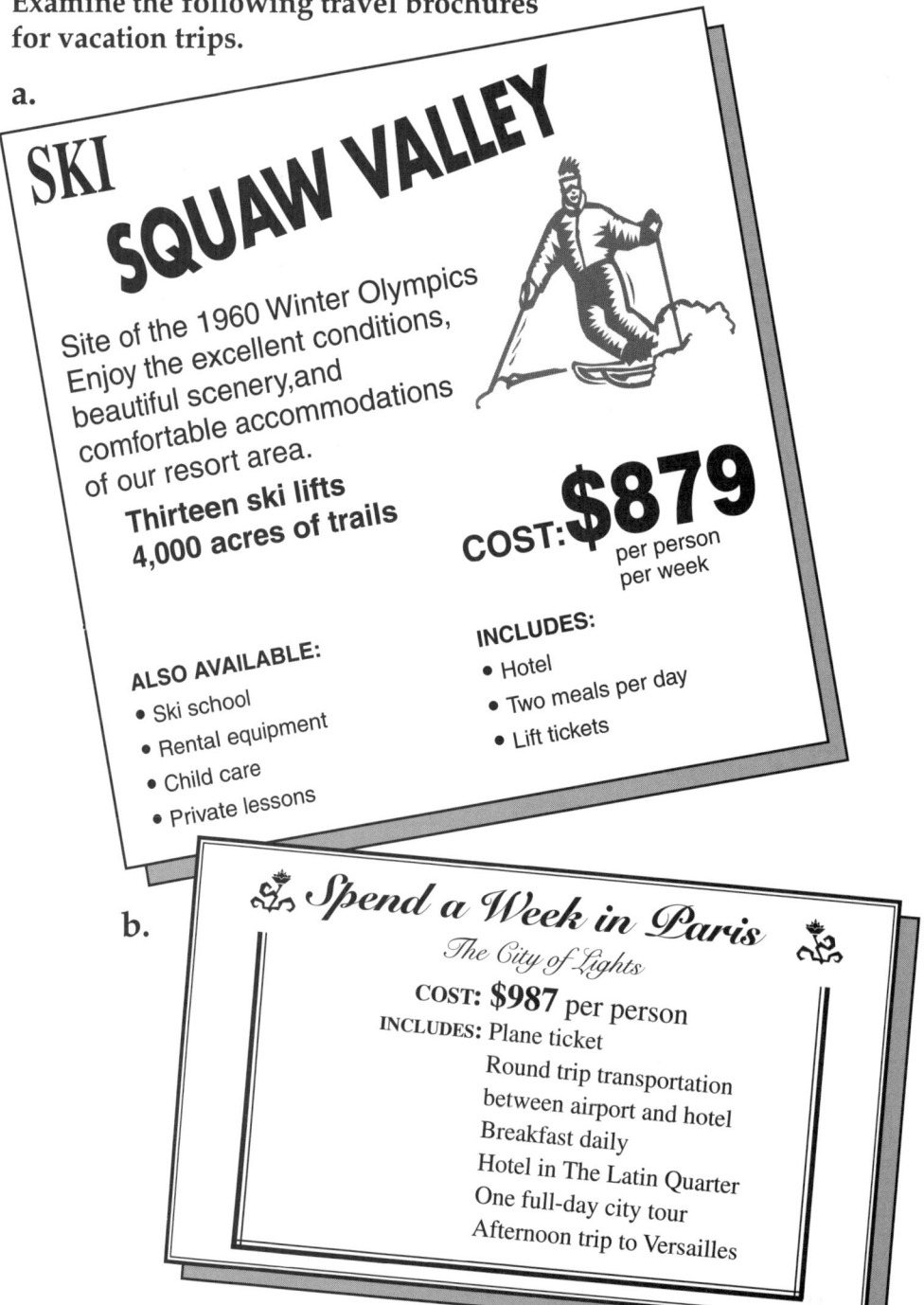

a.

SKI SQUAW VALLEY

Site of the 1960 Winter Olympics Enjoy the excellent conditions, beautiful scenery, and comfortable accommodations of our resort area.

**Thirteen ski lifts
4,000 acres of trails**

COST: $879 per person per week

ALSO AVAILABLE:
- Ski school
- Rental equipment
- Child care
- Private lessons

INCLUDES:
- Hotel
- Two meals per day
- Lift tickets

b.

Spend a Week in Paris
The City of Lights

COST: $987 per person
INCLUDES: Plane ticket
Round trip transportation between airport and hotel
Breakfast daily
Hotel in The Latin Quarter
One full-day city tour
Afternoon trip to Versailles

TRAVEL TALK / **UNIT 1**

c.

CAYMAN ISLANDS
SPEND TWO WEEKS IN PARADISE ON BEAUTIFUL SEVEN MILE BEACH

COST: $1,850 per person

INCLUDES:
- Hotel on beach
- Welcome cocktail party
- Breakfast daily
- Day tour of island
- Bus into town for duty-free shopping

ALSO AVAILABLE FOR RENT:
Scuba diving equipment
Jet skis
Sailboats

SEE YOUR TRAVEL AGENT FOR DETAILS

d.

COME CRUISE WITH US

Travel in style from Ensenada to Hawaii

INCLUDES:
- Ten days on board our luxury ship with three swimming pools
- Three meals daily with midnight buffet
- Casino
- Day trips on Maui and Oahu
- Full gym and spa services
- Activities for children and adults

COST: $2,500

e.

BACK TO NATURE
Private campground in North Carolina. Relax and enjoy the beauty of nature.

COST: $25. per night per campsite

FACILITIES:
Toilets, showers
Hiking trails
Biking trails
Barbecue areas
Public phones

ALSO AVAILABLE:
Boat rentals
Fishing gear
Bicycles

(continued on the next page)

SELECTION 2

Now read the following postcards from people who went on the vacations advertised in the brochures. Match each postcard with the correct vacation trip. Write the name of the vacation trip on the line provided.

1. Dear Donna,
   Hi. This city is so romantic. I think I'm in love. I met the greatest guy on the tour, and we get along so well. Guess what? He's from Los Angeles, too! We've visited at least ten museums and eaten at some wonderful restaurants. I'll tell you all the details when I get back home.
   See you soon,
   Connie

Vacation: _____

2. Dear Barbara,
   We're having a great time. So far, we've had perfect snow every day, and it's not TOO cold. The kids are taking ski lessons in the mornings and skiing with us in the afternoons. No broken bones yet! Our chalet is nice, but quite small. Next year you and Mike should come with us.
   Take care,
   Rachel

Vacation: _____

TRAVEL TALK / **UNIT 1**

3. Dear Mom and Dad,
   I was seasick the first day, but now I'm fine and having a wonderful time. There are lots of activities and we are busy all day. There's even a casino on board, and I won $50 last night. The food is fantastic, and there's so much of it—I'm sure I've gained ten pounds. We'll be home in two days. I'll call you then.

   Love,
   Betsy

Vacation: _____
_____

4. Dear Larry,
   The first week flew by. This is the most relaxing vacation ever! The beaches are beautiful and our hotel is perfect. Lynn got sunburned the first day, but now she's using lots of sunblock. We've met some nice people, and we usually have dinner with them. We'll probably be home by the time you get this, so I'll talk to you soon.

   So long,
   Gary

Vacation: _____
_____

5. Dear Kathy,
   This is not my idea of a great time. Greg and the kids love it, but I'm miserable. Now I realize how much I like hotels and hot showers. I'm covered with mosquito bites and I hate cooking over a campfire. At least it hasn't rained, and the kids are getting lots of exercise hiking. Only two more days until we can go home and sleep in real beds!

   Love,
   Robby

Vacation: _____
_____

17

SELECTION 3

If you have done much flying across time zones, you have probably experienced jet lag. In **Flying High, but Feeling Low,** you will read about some of the causes and symptoms of jet lag and ways to prevent it.

BEFORE YOU READ

PREREADING ACTIVITIES

A. Answer these questions about your general comfort during and after airplane trips. Check YES or NO.

1. After a long trip on an airplane, do you feel tired, weak, sick, or confused?

    YES ____   NO ____

2. Do you continue to feel this way for several days after the flight?

    YES ____   NO ____

3. Do you have trouble eating or sleeping after a long plane trip?

    YES ____   NO ____

4. Do you ever feel thirsty or dizzy during air travel?

    YES ____   NO ____

5. Do you feel different after a north-to-south trip than you do after an east-to-west trip?

    YES ____   NO ____

B. Before you read the article, discuss the meanings of the following words with your teacher and classmates.

confused	stress	fatigue
symptoms	time zones	concentrate
suffer	flexible	rigid

Flying High, but Feeling Low

1. Do you ever feel sick, confused, or very tired after a long plane ride? If you were flying east to west or west to east, the problem could have been jet lag. Jet lag happens when your body's time clock becomes confused. Crossing several time zones may make you feel very tired. You may become confused because you are fatigued. In fact, you may become so mixed-up that you won't be able to concentrate. You might get headaches and notice that you have problems eating and sleeping. These are all symptoms of jet lag.

2. However, if you feel tired after flying from north to south or south to north, you do not have jet lag. You probably feel tired from the stress and work of getting ready for the trip. You will feel better after you get some sleep. The symptoms that you feel during a flight, such as thirst and motion sickness, are not jet lag either. They are caused by the air pressure in the plane. When you travel north or south you do not change time zones. Therefore, you do not have true jet lag.

SELECTION 3

3   Some people suffer more from jet lag than other people do. Symptoms may last for one day or several days. Chronobiologists, the scientists who study the effects of time on living things, say that the seriousness of your reaction depends on several factors. One factor is the number of time zones you crossed. Another factor is whether you flew east to west or west to east. It is easier to adjust after an east-to-west flight. Personality factors also affect how easily you adapt to the new time. For example, "night" people adapt more easily than "morning" people. Extroverts (outgoing, sociable people) adjust more easily than introverts (shy, quiet people). Flexible people who don't mind changes have fewer problems than inflexible people who are rigid and don't like change. Younger people suffer less than older people. Healthier people get over jet lag more easily than people who are sick.

4   Jet lag is something that many people feel but not many understand. Researchers are working to understand jet lag well enough to be able to prevent it. To avoid serious symptoms, it may help to drink plenty of liquids in flight, wear comfortable clothes, and move around every hour. Some doctors even recommend special diets to help control jet lag. Books and anti-jetlag products are already available in stores. If you are planning to fly across time zones, don't let jet lag ruin your trip.

●●●●●●●●●●●●●●●●●●●●●

HOW WELL DID YOU READ?

A. Circle the letter in front of the best answer to each question.

1. Flying in which direction is more likely to cause jet lag?

   a. north to south
   b. west to east
   c. east to west

2. Which of the following is *not* a symptom of jet lag?

   a. motion sickness
   b. headaches
   c. eating problems

3. Which of the following is *not* mentioned as a way to avoid jet lag?

   a. drinking liquids and moving around
   b. wearing comfortable clothes
   c. avoiding salty food

4. Who usually suffers less from jet lag?

   a. "morning people"
   b. introverts
   c. flexible people

5. Which of the following does *not* affect jet lag?

   a. the number of time zones you crossed
   b. air pressure in the plane
   c. personality factors

B. Answer the following questions in the space provided.

1. What causes jet lag?

2. What are some of the common symptoms of jet lag? Make a list.

3. Why do some people suffer from jet lag more than others?

4. What are some things you can do to control jet lag?

The world's busiest airport is Chicago's O'Hare International Airport. It averages 2,300 takeoffs and landings per day, one every fifty-four seconds.

SELECTION 3

EXPANDING VOCABULARY

Complete each sentence with a word from the list.

rigid   extrovert   symptoms
time zones   flexible   introvert

1. Dana likes to go out a lot and be with other people. She is an _____.

2. Peter doesn't like to make changes in his life. He keeps to a schedule and never wants to change his plans. He is _____.

3. The Browns flew from Boston to London. They crossed several _____.

4. Steve is not very social. He likes to be alone and rarely goes out to do things with other people. He is an _____.

5. Jane adjusts well to changes in her life. She travels a lot and doesn't mind changes in her schedule. She is _____.

6. Mark feels sick. He has the flu. He told the doctor he had a fever, a sore throat, and a headache. The fever, sore throat, and headache are _____ of the flu.

BUILDING VOCABULARY SKILLS

SYNONYMS AND ANTONYMS

Decide if the following pairs of words are synonyms or antonyms. If they are synonyms, circle S. If they are antonyms, circle A.

1. tired	fatigued	S	A
2. confused	mixed-up	S	A
3. introvert	extrovert	S	A
4. sick	healthy	S	A
5. adjust	adapt	S	A
6. rigid	flexible	S	A

TYING IT ALL TOGETHER

TRAVEL TALK / **UNIT 1**

DISCUSSION

1. For some people, the best part of traveling is returning home. Is this true for you? Why or why not?

2. Many people believe that traveling makes you more open-minded. When you travel to other places, you see how different kinds of people live, act, and think. Do you agree with this idea? In what ways has traveling made you more open-minded?

3. Mark Twain, an American author, once said, "Travel is fatal to prejudice, bigotry, and narrow-mindedness." Benjamin Disraeli, a British statesman and author, said something similar: "Travel teaches toleration." Discuss the meanings of these two quotes.

JUST FOR FUN
THE NAME GAME

Write the letters of your first name on the lines provided. Then write the name of at least one country that begins with each letter in your name. Follow the example.

J	Japan
I	Iran
M	Mexico
___	_____
___	_____
___	_____
___	_____
___	_____
___	_____
___	_____
___	_____
___	_____

Are there students in your class from any of the countries you chose?

TYING IT ALL TOGETHER

CLASS PROJECT
TRAVEL MAGAZINE

Choose a place in your country that you think people in your class would like to visit. Write a short description of the place for your classmates. Try to include some pictures and interesting facts. Put your description and pictures together with those of your classmates. Make enough copies for everyone in your class. Think of a title for your class travel magazine and have someone design a cover for it.

VOCABULARY REVIEW
WORK TOGETHER

In small groups, discuss the meaning of each of the following words from this unit. Write a definition or a synonym for each word. Try not to use your dictionary. Then, as a group, write a sentence for each word that shows you understand the meaning of the word. Share your sentences with the rest of the class.

1. occasionally _____

2. companion _____

3. wander _____

4. experience _____

5. realize _____

6. worried _____

7. fortunately _____

8. confused _____

TRAVEL TALK / **UNIT 1**

9. symptom _____

_____

10. fatigue _____

_____

11. adapt _____

_____

12. flexible _____

_____

13. rigid _____

_____

SELF-TEST

Complete the letters with words from the lists.

1. worried   realized   weekend
   confused   companion   fortunately
   experience   wandered

Dear Kazuo,

   I have been in Philadelphia for two weeks now. It's very different from Tokyo. The university is huge. I spent the first _____ trying to find out where everything was. I _____ around for two days. My only _____ was my roommate, Paula, from Peru. She is very nice, but she was just as _____ as I was. We kept getting lost! We were both _____ about starting classes. Everything seemed so new and different.

(continued on the next page)

TYING IT ALL TOGETHER

_____, our fears ended as soon as classes began. We _____ that all the other students were friendly and just as nervous as we were.

The classes are very interesting, and I'm learning a lot. We have homework every day, but we still have time to explore the city. I'm sure that studying English in the United States will be a wonderful _____. Why don't you come next semester? I know you'd love it, too.

                       Love,
                       Keiko Suzuki

2. | rigid | symptoms | adjust |
   | occasionally | flexible | fatigue |

Dear Advisor,

I consider myself to be a very _____ person. I don't mind changes and I _____ well to new situations. On the other hand, my husband, Cliff, is very _____. He hates any kind of change. We live in California. _____, we fly to New York to visit our friends there. Cliff always suffers from jet lag on these trips. He gets all the usual _____, but the worst is _____. For the first few days he is too tired to do anything. What can you suggest to help him?

                       From,
                       Worried Wife

TRAVEL TALK / **UNIT 1**

READER'S JOURNAL

At the end of every unit in this book, you will write for ten to twenty minutes. This is called a *reader's journal*. The purpose of the reader's journal is to help you think about the topic of each unit and tie together your thoughts. When you write in your journal, you should choose something that interests you. You don't need to worry about spelling, grammar, and punctuation. Just try to write as much as you can in English without translating from your native language.

Since this unit is about travel, the theme of your journal should have something to do with travel. Choose one of the topics from the list, or pick a topic of your own to write about.

- the best or worst trip you have ever taken
- why you like or don't like to travel
- advice for someone traveling to your country
- your thoughts on one of the questions from the Points to Ponder or Tying It All Together sections

READER'S JOURNAL

Date: _____

Attitudes About Animals

FYI Unit·2

Selections

1. All for the Love of Fritz 31

2. Can Animals Think? .39

3. Anti-Fur Groups Renew Fur Debate 45

There are so many animals in the world today that it is impossible to count them. In fact, we do not even know how many kinds of animals there are. Although scientists have counted and named over a million types of animals, hundreds of new kinds are discovered each year. As you read the articles in this unit, think about your attitudes toward animals.

POINTS TO PONDER

Answer each of the following questions about yourself. Then discuss your answers in small groups.

1. In your country, is it common for people to keep animals as pets? If so, what animals are popular as pets? Do people usually keep their pets inside their home or outdoors?

2. Do you have any pets now? Have you ever had a pet? What kind? If you have a pet, do you consider it as a member of your family?

3. Is it the responsibility of humans to protect animals? Why or why not? How can we best protect them?

SELECTION 1

ATTITUDES ABOUT ANIMALS / **UNIT 2**

Doris Davis is a wonderful storyteller. Animals have always been an important part of her life, and she loves to tell stories about the pets she has had. One of her favorite animals was a pony named Fritz that her father bought in 1915. When you read the following interview with Ms. Davis, **All for the Love of Fritz,** you will understand why she is known as such a great storyteller.

BEFORE YOU READ

PREREADING ACTIVITY

Before you read the interview, look at the picture of Doris Davis and her pony Fritz. What can you tell from the picture about their relationship?

All for the Love of Fritz

What can you tell us about Fritz?

1   In 1915, when I was eleven years old, my father bought me a pony named Fritz. He was small, about four feet tall. He lived in his own little house that my uncle built in our backyard. Over the years, Fritz really became one of the family. Fritz was not an ordinary pony. In fact, he was very unusual in many ways.

2   I was not the first person who owned Fritz. He was originally owned by an actress named

Fritzy Sheff. Fritz performed with her on stage. He used to "dance" with Ms. Sheff while she sang and he even "bowed" at the end of songs. He loved it when people in the audience clapped. He would put his front foot out just like he was taking a bow. Even when Fritz lived with me, he would always begin to dance whenever he heard music.

I'm sure you have some favorite stories about Fritz. Tell us the one you like the best.

3   To understand one of my favorite stories, you have to know that my family owned a very big car. It was a convertible. When the top was down, Fritz could fit into the back of the car. Since Fritz loved ice cream, we always took him with us when we went out for ice cream. You can imagine the looks we got from the people who saw us driving down the street with a pony on the back seat eating an ice cream cone!

Can you remember any other funny stories about your life with Fritz?

4   My mother was always asking me if I had brushed my teeth. After every meal she would say, "Did you brush your teeth?" Every time I had a snack, just some cookies or a piece of fruit, she wanted to know if I had brushed my teeth. I decided that Fritz should have clean teeth too. Naturally, I thought I should clean them for him. So, I got out my toothbrush and toothpaste and brushed his teeth. Fritz just loved it. He would pull his lips back so I could brush real well. Then, I would put more toothpaste on my brush and begin again. Fritz would roll the toothpaste around in his mouth. He was so happy when I brushed his teeth.

5   I decided to ask my father if it was okay for Fritz to swallow toothpaste. He asked, "What have you been doing to that pony?" I explained that it was very important to have clean teeth and that Fritz needed me to help him brush his teeth. My father was upset. He said I was making a baby out of Fritz. Then he asked me what toothbrush I used on the pony. When I told him that I used my own toothbrush he said, "What??! You are never to use your toothbrush on that pony again. Your mother will get you a new one."

6   We had many different pets when I was growing up, but Fritz was definitely the most interesting. I don't know about animals in general, but *mine* have always been *very* intelligent.

ATTITUDES ABOUT ANIMALS / **UNIT 2**

HOW WELL DID YOU READ?

Read the following statements. If a statement is true, write *T* on the line. If it is false, write *F*.

_____ 1. Doris Davis was the first person who owned Fritz.

_____ 2. Fritz loved to perform.

_____ 3. Fritz was too big to fit in the family car.

_____ 4. One of Fritz's favorite foods was ice cream.

_____ 5. Doris's parents wanted her to brush Fritz's teeth every day.

_____ 6. Fritz lived in a little house that Doris's uncle had built.

_____ 7. Fritz was the only pet that Doris had when she was growing up.

BUILDING READING SKILLS

LOCATING INFORMATION

Doris Davis discusses many things about her favorite pet, Fritz. Look through the interview to find where she talks about each of the following topics. Then, in the space provided, write the number of the paragraph where each of the following topics is discussed.

1. Fritz's trips in the family car to get ice cream (¶ _____)

2. Doris loved to brush Fritz's teeth. (¶ _____)

3. the house that Fritz lived in (¶ _____)

4. Fritz's life before Doris owned him (¶ _____)

5. her father's reaction to Doris brushing Fritz's teeth (¶ _____)

FIGURE IT OUT

VOCABULARY IN CONTEXT

As your vocabulary and skills in English improve, you will be able to figure out the meanings of new words from the context of the sentence or paragraph. Sometimes you will find a synonym, an antonym, or a definition of a difficult word right in the reading.

Example: *Fritz was not an <u>ordinary</u> pony. In fact, he was very unusual in many ways.*

What do you think <u>ordinary</u> means?

  a. big
  (b.) usual
  c. young

(continued on the next page)

SELECTION 1

With a partner, try to guess the meaning of each underlined word. Use the information in the sentences to figure out the meaning. Do not use your dictionary. Circle the letter of the word or phrase that is closest in meaning to the underlined words in the following sentences.

1. *I'm sure you have some favorite stories about Fritz. Tell us the one you like the best.*

   a. most interesting
   b. very unusual
   c. something you like the best

2. *I was not the first person who owned Fritz. He was originally owned by an actress named Fritzy Sheff.*

   a. first
   b. best
   c. next

3. *... my family owned a very big car. It was a convertible. When the top was down, Fritz could fit into the back of the car.*

   a. a very big car
   b. a car whose top can go down
   c. a fast sports car

4. *Every time I had a snack, just some cookies or a piece of fruit, she wanted to know if I had brushed my teeth.*

   a. a toothache
   b. a big dinner
   c. a little something to eat

5. *My father was upset. . . . When I told him that I used my own toothbrush he said, "What??! You are never to use your toothbrush on that pony again. . . ."*

   a. disturbed
   b. happy
   c. hungry

It is estimated that there are more than 75 million horses in the world and more than 400 million dogs.

BUILDING READING SKILLS
SCANNING FOR DETAILS

We read for several different reasons:

- for pleasure
- for specific information
- for general knowledge

We also read in different ways. The way we read depends on our purpose. For example, when the purpose is to find specific information, it is not necessary to read every word carefully. Often we read quickly, looking for a specific piece of information. This is called **scanning.** An important part of scanning is knowing what kind of information to look for.

A. Read the questions below about the number of pets in the United States. Then scan the paragraph that follows to find the information you need to answer the questions. Work as quickly as possible. You do not have to read the whole paragraph.

1. How many cats do Americans own as pets? _____

   _____

2. How many pet dogs are there in the United States? _____

   _____

3. How many more pet birds are there in the United States than

   horses? _____

Pets are very popular in the United States. In fact, Americans own 57 million cats as pets. This favorite is followed by dogs. Americans have 52.5 million pet dogs. Birds and horses are also popular pets in the United States. Americans have 11.7 million pet birds and 4.9 million horses.[1]

---

[1] Source: U.S. Bureau of the Census, *Statistical Abstract of the United States, 1994.* 114th Edition. (Washington, D.C., 1994).

SELECTION 1

B. Now answer these questions about the percentage of households in the United States that have pets. Do not read the following paragraph carefully, just look for the information you need to answer the questions. Work as quickly as possible.

1. What percent of American households have dogs as pets?

   _____

2. What percent of American households have cats as pets?

   _____

3. What percent of households in the United States have pet birds?

   _____

4. What percent have horses?

   _____

Americans love pets. In fact, over half of the households in the United States have pets. In the United States, 36.5 percent of the households have dogs for pets. This percentage is followed by the percentage of households that own cats: 30.9 percent of households have cats as pets. Birds and horses are also common choices for pets: 5.7 percent of the households in the United States have pet birds and 2 percent have horses.[2]

Complete the chart with the correct percentages.

Pets	Percentage of U.S. Households
Dogs	
Cats	
Birds	
Horses	

[2] Source: U.S. Bureau of the Census, *Statistical Abstract of the United States, 1994*. 114th edition. (Washington, D.C., 1994).

ATTITUDES ABOUT ANIMALS / **UNIT 2**

C. Practice your scanning skills with the following longer article, "Crazy about Cats or Just Crazy?" Read each question and scan the article for the information you need to answer it. Look for key words to help you find the information. Stop reading as soon as you locate the answer and go on to the next question. Work as quickly as possible.

1. What percent of cat owners talk to their cats the way they talk to children? _____

2. What percent of cat owners said that their cats knew some tricks?
   _____

3. What percent of cat owners consider their cats a member of the family? _____

4. What percent give their cats a birthday party? _____

5. What percent of cat owners speak to their cats at least once a day?
   _____

Crazy about Cats or Just Crazy?

[1] Many people who do not own a cat think that cats are not as friendly and interesting as dogs. However, people who do own cats think that they are very friendly, fascinating, and loving pets. Victoria Voith studies animal behavior at the University of Pennsylvania. She asked 887 cat owners to fill out a questionnaire about their cats. The results of her survey may surprise you.

37

2   Almost all cat owners think of their cat as a part of the family. In fact, 96 percent said that they consider their pet cat a family member. Many said that their cat sleeps on their bed, wakes them up in the morning, comes to greet them when they come home from work, and acts as a "watch cat" when a stranger comes into the house.

3   Birthdays are important for cat owners. About 70 percent said that they give their cat a present for his or her birthday. A few (6 percent) even give the cat a birthday party.

4   Most cat owners talk to their cats. More than 95 percent responded that they speak to the cat at least once a day. About 40 percent of the respondents said that they talk to their cats the way they talk to children. Twenty percent said they talk to their cats just like they would talk to an adult. And about 35 percent said they talk to their cats as pets. Finally, thirteen percent responded that they speak to their cats in all three ways. In other words, they speak to the cat as a child, an adult, or a pet. It all depends on the circumstances.

5   Cat owners seem to have a special connection with their pets. More than 70 percent said that they are usually aware of their cats' moods. Over half of the respondents think that their cat is usually aware of their moods.

6   People usually associate dogs with doing tricks. However, 40 percent of the cat owners who were surveyed said that their cats know some tricks. Popular tricks include fetching, meowing, sitting, and rolling on command.

7   The results of the questionnaire clearly indicate that cat owners feel very close to their cats. Are they crazy about cats, or are they just plain crazy? What do you think?

SELECTION 2

ATTITUDES ABOUT ANIMALS / UNIT 2

Have you ever wondered if animals can really think? Do you believe they have emotions similar to those of humans? **Can Animals Think?** discusses the observations and opinions of scientists who are studying animal behavior.

BEFORE YOU READ

PREREADING DISCUSSION

1. What do you think are some of the major differences between humans and other animals?

2. Have you ever had a pet that you thought was very smart? Why? Describe your pet's behavior.

3. Do you think animals can have a sense of humor? Are they capable of emotions such as love, anger, and fear? Discuss your ideas with your classmates.

Can Animals Think?

1   Can animals really think? Can they make decisions based on information? For years, scientists have debated these questions. Now, many of them believe that some animals have the brain power to understand new situations, make decisions, and plan ahead. The following are just a few of the many examples of animal intelligence that scientists have observed.

2   Dandy is a young male chimpanzee at the Wisconsin Regional Primate Center. Recently, he did something that surprised scientists there. The scientists had buried some grapefruit in the sand. Dandy knew where the grapefruit was, but when the other chimps were in the area, Dandy pretended that he did not know the location. Later, when the other chimps fell asleep, Dandy went right to the spot where the grapefruit was hidden, dug it up, and ate it. Amazingly, Dandy was able to plan ahead and trick his friends.

3   A green-backed female heron[1] in Japan also did something surprising. She invented a new, creative way to get her food. When she saw some minnows[2] swimming around in a pond, she came up with a way to catch some. First, she found a twig and broke it into small pieces. Then, she took it to the pond and put it in the water. She even moved it to a place in the pond where it would attract the minnows. Finally, when the minnows swam over to the twig, she was able to catch one for her lunch. This shows how the heron was able to make and use a tool.

4   At the University of Arizona, a gray parrot named Alex surprised his trainer, Irene Pepperberg. She has been working with Alex for 15 years, teaching him to talk, name and count objects, and answer simple questions about them. He is very good at these tasks. He even says, "I'm sorry" when he makes a mistake answering a question. But what Alex once did outside of the laboratory was even more impressive. When he had to go to the veterinarian's office for lung surgery, he became upset. As Pepperberg started to leave, Alex said, "Come here. I love you. I'm sorry. I want to go back." Alex thought he was being punished for doing something wrong. He seemed able to use language to express his thoughts.

5   A gorilla named Timmy, who had lived alone for most of his life, provided another unusual example of animal behavior. Timmy was brought to the Bronx Zoo in New York to mate with Pattycake, a female gorilla who lived at the zoo. After their baby was born, it became sick and the mother and baby were taken away. The head of the zoo reported that Timmy became very upset when they left. He wouldn't eat or sleep. He even cried. He looked everywhere to see if Pattycake had returned. It certainly seemed like he had fallen in love.

6   In Italy, scientists showed that an octopus could learn how to perform a task by watching another octopus do it. In this experiment, an octopus who did not know how to open a jar to get to a

---

1 green-backed heron A bird with long legs and a long neck and bill that lives near water.
2 minnow Small, freshwater fish.

crab inside was allowed to watch another octopus who did know how. After observing how the second octopus did it, the first octopus was able to open the jar himself. Until recently, many scientists had thought that only mammals could learn by watching others.

7   Stories like these raise many questions about animals and the way they think and behave. It seems that animals are capable of more than just processing information like a robot. Perhaps their behavior is the result of more than just instinct[3] and memorized rules. Based on these observations, more scientists are concluding that animals really can think. What do you think?

[3] **instinct** A natural or inborn force that causes animals to act. It is not based on mental ability or learning.

BUILDING READING SKILLS
RECALLING FACTS

The article describes the unusual behavior of five animals: a chimpanzee, a heron, a parrot, an octopus, and a gorilla. Complete the chart below with the facts from the following list:

lives at the Bronx Zoo	used a twig as a tool
lives in Wisconsin	learned how to open a jar
fell in love	tricked other animals
lives in Arizona	lives in Japan
can count objects	became a father
eats crabs	likes grapefruit
eats minnows	used language to express thoughts
can talk	lives in Italy

Dandy, the chimp	The green-backed heron	Alex, the parrot	Timmy, the gorilla	The octopus

SELECTION 2

BUILDING READING SKILLS
IDENTIFYING MAIN IDEAS

Summarize the main idea of each story by completing the following sentences.

1. Dandy was able to _____
   _____

2. A heron in Japan used a _____
   _____

3. A parrot named Alex _____
   _____

4. Timmy showed unusual behavior by _____
   _____

5. An octopus in Italy _____
   _____

TALK IT OVER
DISCUSSION

Some people believe that only humans are capable of real thinking. They feel that this is what separates humans from the rest of the animal kingdom. Other people believe that, like humans, some animals have the ability to think and understand.

Read the following list. Put a check mark next to the ideas that you agree with. Discuss your opinions with your classmates.

_____ 1. Animals are capable of planning ahead.

_____ 2. The way humans use their minds is very different from the way animals use their minds.

_____ 3. It is possible for animals to trick humans and other animals.

_____ 4. Only humans can solve problems.

_____ 5. Studying the way animals behave can help us understand more about the way humans behave.

_____ 6. Mammals are not the only animals capable of learning how to do something by watching.

EXPANDING VOCABULARY

Circle the letter of the word or phrase that is closest in meaning to the underlined word in each sentence.

1. *First, she found a twig and broke it into small pieces.*

    a. rock
    b. stick
    c. grapefruit

2. *. . . Dandy went right to the spot where the grapefruit was hidden, dug it up, and ate it.*

    a. place
    b. circle
    c. letter

3. *The following are just a few of the many examples of animal intelligence that scientists have observed.*

    a. discussed
    b. behaved
    c. seen

4. *He looked everywhere to see if Pattycake had returned.*

    a. come back
    b. fallen asleep
    c. eaten lunch

5. *He is very good at these tasks.*

    a. words
    b. jobs
    c. birds

6. *Recently, he did something that surprised them.*

    a. now
    b. a long time ago
    c. a short time ago

FYI

If intelligence is defined as speed and ability to do tasks, the most intelligent animals after man are: chimpanzee, gorilla, orangutan, baboon, gibbon, monkey, smaller-toothed whale, dolphin, elephant.[1]

---

[1] Research by Edward O. Wilson, in Russell Ash, *Top Ten of Everything*, (New York: Dorling Kindersley), 35.

SELECTION 2

BUILDING VOCABULARY SKILLS

SYNONYMS AND ANTONYMS

Decide if the following pairs of words are synonyms or antonyms. If they are synonyms, circle *S*. If they are antonyms, circle *A*.

1.	surprised	shocked	S	A
2.	asleep	awake	S	A
3.	right	correct	S	A
4.	happened	occurred	S	A
5.	reported	said	S	A
6.	punish	praise	S	A
7.	spot	place	S	A
8.	attract	repel	S	A
9.	upset	calm	S	A
10.	perhaps	maybe	S	A

It was illegal for people to keep dogs as pets in China until December 1994.

SELECTION 3

ATTITUDES ABOUT ANIMALS / UNIT 2

Some people are against wearing animal fur. **Anti-Fur Groups Renew Fur Debate** shows how some animal rights groups[1] are protesting the wearing of fur. These groups are trying to convince people to stop wearing fur because it is unfair to animals.

BEFORE YOU READ

PREREADING ACTIVITY

Look at the pictures that go with the article. What are the people doing? What do the signs say? What do they mean?

Read the article and do the exercises that follow.

Anti-Fur Groups Renew Fur Debate

[1] **animal rights groups** People who work to protect animals and their rights.

1. A billboard in Hollywood, California, shows model Christy Turlington nude. The caption reads, "I'd rather go naked than wear fur."

2. The billboard is part of new efforts by anti-fur groups. They want to convince women not to wear fur. But the fur industry is fighting back.

3. One of the best-known anti-fur groups is People for Ethical Treatment of Animals (PETA). It says that animals are mistreated to make furs.

4. PETA's booklets show animals in dirty cages. And it says fur farmers kill animals in cruel ways.

5. But a fur farmers' group says they have to treat the animals well. Tim Sullivan is the group's animal welfare director. "The only way you can produce quality fur is to produce quality care," he said.

6. PETA also says that wild animals suffer when caught in traps. But trappers say the traps kill quickly.

7. The two sides can't even agree on how many people are buying furs. The Fur Information Council of America is a group of businesses that make and sell furs. It says sales were up 10 percent in 1992.

8. PETA claims that fur sales are down. It says it has convinced many women to stop wearing fur.

9. But people in the fur business say PETA doesn't have that much power. They argue that sales depend more on the economy and the weather.

10. The conflict often ends up on the sidewalk. Debbie Leahy says she wants to end animal suffering. She confronts women who wear furs. She says they are vain and selfish.

11. But fur wearers don't agree. And they are tired of the activists.

12. "I can wear anything I want," said one woman. "Why don't these people put their efforts into working for the homeless, or abused children, or something really important?"

BUILDING READING SKILLS
UNDERSTANDING POINTS OF VIEW

The article discusses the two sides of the fur debate. PETA has one point of view and the fur industry has a very different one. The chart below summarizes the two sides of the issue.

Read the information presented in the chart. Then, fill in the empty boxes with a statement that expresses the opposing point of view.

PETA	Fur Industry
1.	1. You can only produce good fur if you treat animals well.
2. Wild animals suffer when they are caught in traps.	2.
3.	3. Fur sales rose 10 percent in 1992.
4. PETA has convinced many women to stop wearing fur.	4.
5.	5. People can wear anything they want.

SELECTION 3

FIGURE IT OUT
VOCABULARY IN CONTEXT

Without using your dictionary, guess the meaning of the underlined words. Circle the letter of the word or phrase that is closest in meaning to the underlined word in each of the following sentences.

1. *They [anti-fur groups] want to <u>convince</u> women not to wear fur.*

    a. persuade
    b. choose
    c. promise

2. *It [PETA] says that animals are <u>mistreated</u> to make furs.*

    a. helped
    b. treated poorly
    c. treated well

3. *It [The Fur Information Council of America] says sales were up 10 percent in 1992. PETA <u>claims</u> that fur sales are down.*

    a. disagrees
    b. helps
    c. says

4. *Debbie Leahy says she wants to end animal <u>suffering</u>.*

    a. pain
    b. hunger
    c. happiness

CLASS ACTIVITY
DISCUSSING OPINIONS

Wearing fur is only one of many controversial issues involving animals. Other issues include hunting endangered animals, eating meat, and using animals for laboratory experiments.

A. In small groups, choose one of these issues and discuss your point of view.

B. With your partners, make a chart that summarizes the two sides of the issue.

C. Put your charts on the chalkboard and explain them to the rest of the class.

TYING IT ALL TOGETHER

ATTITUDES ABOUT ANIMALS / **UNIT 2**

DISCUSSION

1. "Animals are such agreeable friends—they ask no questions, they pass no criticism."[1] What does this statement mean? Do you think this is the reason so many people have pets?

2. Explain the following statement, "The more I see of men, the more I like dogs!" Is this also true for you?

3. Thousands of species of wild animals are becoming endangered.[2] There are many reasons wild animals are disappearing so fast. Name some endangered animals, and make a list of some of the reasons they are disappearing.

_____
_____
_____
_____
_____
_____
_____
_____
_____
_____
_____
_____

4. Humans can contribute to the serious problem of animal extinction. They can also help to solve it. Can you think of some of the ways that humans are making the problem worse? What do you think we can do to prevent the problem from becoming more serious? How can we protect our animals?

[1] George Eliot, *Scenes of Clerical Life, Mr. Gilfil's Love Story*.
[2] **Endangered species** Animals whose ability to survive is in danger.

49

TYING IT ALL TOGETHER

5. Proverbs are well-known sayings and expressions. Many English proverbs are about animals. Read the following proverbs and think about their meanings. Then match each proverb with the correct explanation.

PROVERB

_____ 1. Curiosity killed the cat.

_____ 2. When the cat's away, the mice will play.

_____ 3. The early bird catches the worm.

_____ 4. You can't teach an old dog new tricks.

_____ 5. Don't count your chickens before they hatch.

_____ 6. Birds of a feather flock together.

_____ 7. A bird in the hand is worth two in the bush.

_____ 8. You can lead a horse to water, but you can't make it drink.

_____ 9. Let sleeping dogs lie.

_____ 10. His bark is worse than his bite.

EXPLANATION

a. You can make a suggestion, but you can't force someone to do something.

b. You can get into a lot of trouble if you ask too many questions.

c. It's better to have one thing for sure than the possibility of two.

d. His actions are not as strong as his words.

e. Starting early leads to success.

f. Don't plan on something until it's definite.

g. People don't work as hard when the boss is not there.

h. Similar people tend to find each other.

i. As people become older, it becomes harder to get them to change.

j. Leave things the way they are; don't start problems.

Make a list of proverbs in your language that use animals. Then explain them to your classmates.

_____
_____
_____
_____
_____
_____

JUST FOR FUN

ANIMAL GROUPS

The English language has many names to describe groups, especially groups of animals. For example, a group of birds is called a *flock*. See if you can figure out which word is used to describe each of the following groups of animals. You may need to use a dictionary or ask an English-speaking friend. Then check your answers in the Answer Key on page 209.

bed	colony	mob	band
pack	pride	school	swarm
flock	herd	team	troop

1. _____ of ants
2. _____ of kangaroos
3. _____ of fish
4. _____ of lions
5. _____ of bees
6. _____ of monkeys
7. _____ of sheep or geese
8. _____ of wolves
9. _____ of clams
10. _____ of elephants
11. _____ of ducks or horses
12. _____ of gorillas

TYING IT ALL TOGETHER

ANIMAL EQUATIONS

Have you ever added and subtracted letters instead of numbers? Consider the following example.

Example:

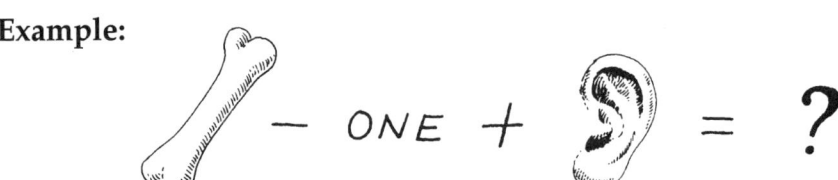

The first picture is a picture of a bone, so we print the letters, B-O-N-E. We are told to subtract O-N-E from B-O-N-E, so we cross out O-N-E, which leaves only the B. Next, we must add E-A-R. When we do this, we get the word B-E-A-R. Bear is the animal that solves the equation.

Now try each of the following. Then check your answers in the Answer Key on page 209.

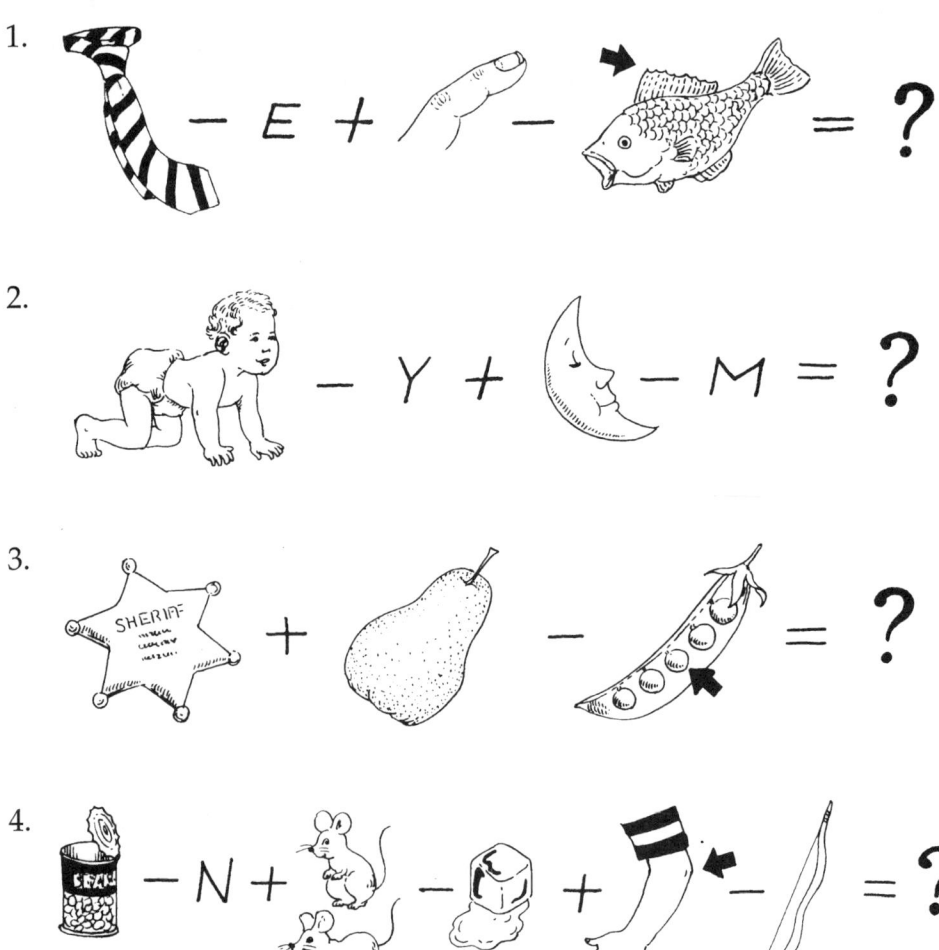

ATTITUDES ABOUT ANIMALS / **UNIT 2**

VOCABULARY REVIEW
WORK TOGETHER

In small groups, discuss the meaning of each of the following words from this unit. Write a definition or a synonym for each word. Try not to use your dictionary. Then, as a group, write a sentence for each word that shows you understand the meaning of the word. Share your sentences with the rest of the class.

1. convince _____

2. claim _____

3. suffer _____

4. shocked _____

5. praise _____

6. twig _____

7. upset _____

8. tasks _____

9. recently _____

(continued on the next page)

TYING IT ALL TOGETHER

10. ordinary _____
_____

11. performance _____
_____

12. favorite _____
_____

13. convertible _____
_____

14. imagine _____
_____

15. snack _____
_____

SELF-TEST

Complete the sentences with words from the lists.

1. task   performs   praised

   When a child _____ a _____ well, she should be _____.

2. snacks   recently   convinced

   Jean has gained a lot of weight _____. I am _____ it is because she eats too many _____.

3. convertible   shocked   ordinary

   I was _____ when I saw Fran's new car. It is not an _____ car. It is a bright pink _____.

4. claims   favorite   imagine

   Kate _____ to have very good taste in clothes. But you can

   _____ the looks she got when she wore her

   _____ dress to the party last night. It was too short, too

   tight, and the colors were horrible.

5. fur   claims   upset

   Suzanne was very _____ when her friend bought a

   _____ coat. She _____ that animals suffer when

   their fur is used for clothing.

READER'S JOURNAL

Think about the topics and ideas you have read about and discussed in this unit. Choose a topic and write about it for ten to twenty minutes. You may pick a topic from the following list or choose one of your own.

- a story about a pet you have had
- your opinion about endangered animals
- your thoughts on using animals in laboratory experiments
- your ideas about animal intelligence
- your thoughts on one of the questions from the Points to Ponder or Tying It All Together Sections

TYING IT ALL TOGETHER

READER'S JOURNAL

Date: _____

FACING CHALLENGES

FYI Unit•3

Selections

1. 86-Year-Old Man in Marathon for 63rd Time . . .59
2. Disabled People Find Challenge on the Slopes . .63
3. Sounds of Bali 67
4. "Dreams" by Langston Hughes 71

All of us face challenges of one kind or another at various points in our lives. In this unit, you will read about three people who faced difficult challenges. As you read the articles, think about the kind of challenge each person faced.

POINTS TO PONDER

Answer each of the following questions about yourself. Then discuss your answers in small groups.

1. What are some challenges that you have faced in the last five years?

   _____

   _____

2. How did you meet each challenge?

   _____

   _____

3. List the goals you have for your future. What challenges will you have to face?

   _____

   _____

4. Look at the cartoon. What do you think it means? Do you think it is funny? Why or why not?

Shoe by Jeff McNelly

Reprinted by permission: Tribune Media Services.

SELECTION 1

FACING CHALLENGES / **UNIT 3**

The Boston Marathon is the oldest race of its kind in the world. It is held every year on the third Monday in April. The winners take approximately two hours to run the 26-mile race. The weather in Boston in April is unpredictable. Some years it is very hot; other years it is cold. This makes it hard for the runners to train for the day of the race. They don't know what kind of conditions to expect.

Approximately 9,000 runners started in the 1994 Boston Marathon. Why would anyone want the torture of running for twenty-six miles? Read the following article, **86-Year-Old Man in Marathon for 63rd Time,** and you will find out.

BEFORE YOU READ

PREREADING DISCUSSION

1. A marathon is a twenty-six-mile race. Have you ever watched or participated in a marathon?

2. Most people who run in marathons must train very hard. What do you think is the best way to prepare for a marathon?

3. Do you participate in any sport that requires a lot of training? If so, how do you prepare for competitions?

Johnny Kelley (center) in Boston Marathon.

SELECTION 1

86-Year-Old Man in Marathon for 63rd Time

1 Johnny Kelley is 86 years old. He has just run the last seven miles of the Boston Marathon. It took him one hour and 15 minutes to run the seven miles. After his run, he went to the medical center to have his blood pressure checked. The nurse was surprised and pleased to see that his blood pressure was 139 over 84. She told him that his blood pressure was "outstanding." Then she said, "I wish mine were that good."

2 Johnny Kelley is known as the great-grandfather of the Boston Marathon. He ran the entire 26 miles of the marathon 61 times. This year was the second time that he has cut back and run only part of it. Kelley holds the record for running more Boston Marathons than anyone else. To honor Kelley, a statue of him has been placed along the marathon route.

3 Thousands of people cheer for him as he runs the course. Today, an 11-year-old boy called out to Kelley, "Hey, Mr. Kelley—you're awesome. Super awesome!" Kelley nods and thanks people as he runs. "It's wonderful," he says. "People come out in the road to shake my hand. I'm cheered by thousands and thousands. I think a lot of them thought I ran the entire race. And maybe they cheered me because they know me after all these years and they don't know the other runners."

● ●

BUILDING READING SKILLS

LOCATING INFORMATION

Scan the background information and the newspaper article for the following facts. HINT: All the answers are numbers.

1. How long is the Boston Marathon?

   _____

2. How many runners started in the 1994 marathon?

   _____

FACING CHALLENGES / **UNIT 3**

3. What was Johnny Kelley's blood pressure after he ran the marathon in 1994?

_____

4. How many times did Mr. Kelley run the entire marathon?

_____

5. How long did it take him to run the last seven miles of the marathon in 1994?

_____

HOW WELL DID YOU READ?

Answer the questions with information from the article.

1. Why is Johnny Kelley known as the great-grandfather of the Boston Marathon? Use information from the article to support your answer.

_____

_____

_____

2. What makes the Boston Marathon such a difficult race to train for?

_____

_____

_____

3. How has Mr. Kelley been honored?

_____

_____

4. What kind of challenges did Johnny Kelley face?

_____

_____

SELECTION 1

FIGURE IT OUT
VOCABULARY IN CONTEXT

Without using your dictionary, try to guess the meaning of the underlined words. Circle the letter of the word or phrase that is closest in meaning to the underlined word in each of the following sentences.

1. *The winners take <u>approximately</u> two hours to run the race. . . . <u>Approximately</u> 9,000 runners started in the 1994 Boston Marathon.*

   a. exactly
   b. about
   c. rarely

2. *The nurse was surprised and pleased to see that his blood pressure was 139 over 84. She told him that his blood pressure was "<u>outstanding</u>." Then she said, "I wish mine were that good."*

   a. very good
   b. terrible
   c. high

In June of 1970, David Kunst of the United States began to walk around the world. He completed his walk in October of 1974, having worn out 21 pairs of shoes. Although many people have tried to walk around the world, Kunst is known to be the first person to have actually completed it.

3. *The weather in Boston in April is <u>unpredictable</u>. Some years it is very hot; other years it is cold.*

   a. very good
   b. hard to know in advance
   c. uninteresting

4. *To <u>honor</u> Kelley, a statue of him has been placed along the marathon route.*

   a. praise
   b. include
   c. hurt

5. *To honor Kelley, a statue of him has been placed along the marathon <u>route</u>.*

   a. year
   b. road
   c. record

EXPANDING VOCABULARY

Cross out the word in each group that does not belong with the other two.

1. approximately   about   exactly
2. torture   honor   pain
3. cheer   cut back   reduce
4. route   course   statue
5. outstanding   excellent   outside

SELECTION 2

FACING CHALLENGES / **UNIT 3**

The following article, **Disabled People Find Challenge on the Slopes,** tells about a football player, Mike Utley, who was seriously hurt during a game. After his injury, he could not move his legs anymore. The article discusses how Utley and others like him were able to overcome their disabilities and find new challenges.

Read the article one time quickly and answer the question that follows.

Disabled People Find Challenge on the Slopes

1. Mike Utley can't move his legs. Yet twice a week, he sails down the ski slopes of Vail, Colorado.
2. Utley was hurt playing football for the Detroit Lions. He lost the use of his legs and some use of his arms. Today he is in a program at Vail for disabled skiers.
3. Utley says skiing gives him a chance to go out and live his life. "Football was everything to me," he says. "I began playing when I was 7 years old. Now Vail has given me a chance to do something else."

SELECTION 2

4   The program's name is Project Challenge. Some of the skiers have problems seeing or hearing. Others have lost limbs or hurt their spines.

5   Utley skis using a device called a bi-ski. It has a seat like a bucket. Utley sits in the seat with his feet up in front of him. Two short, wide skis are on the bottom of the seat. Utley keeps his balance with ski poles. The poles have little ski-shaped pieces on the tips.

6   More than 100 of the 520 U.S. ski resorts have programs for disabled people. The world's biggest program is at the National Sports Center for the Disabled. It is in Winter Park, Colorado.

7   The Winter Park Center conducts research and training. About 3,000 disabled skiers took lessons there last year.

8   The resort at Ski Windham in New York state also serves disabled skiers. Gwen Allard directs disabled skiing there. "There's a neat place in society for a program like ours," says Allard. "You see other people achieve things they never thought they could do."

● ● ● ● ● ● ● ● ● ● ● ● ● ● ● ● ● ● ● ●

CHOOSE THE BEST TITLE

Which of the following do you think would be the best alternative for the title of article?

1. Mike Utley Hurt in Football Game
2. Skiing Programs for the Disabled
3. Special Device for Disabled Skiers Invented

Now read the article again more carefully and do the exercises.

HOW WELL DID YOU READ?

Circle the letter of the word or phrase that best completes each statement.

1. Mike Utley was hurt _____.

   a. while he was skiing
   b. during a football game
   c. at the National Sports Center for the Disabled
   d. while he was playing tennis

2. _____ of the ski resorts in the United States have programs for disabled people.

   a. All
   b. Almost half
   c. About one fifth
   d. A few

3. Some of the skiers in Project Challenge _____.

   a. have problems seeing or hearing
   b. have hurt their spines
   c. have lost arms or legs
   d. all of the above

4. The Winter Park Center _____.

   a. conducts research and training for disabled people
   b. is directed by Gwen Allard
   c. is in Vail, Colorado
   d. none of the above

EXPANDING VOCABULARY

Match each word in column A with the word or phrase in column B that has a similar meaning. Write the correct letter on the line.

	A		B
_____	1. chance	a.	arms and legs
_____	2. twice	b.	injured
_____	3. limbs	c.	teaching
_____	4. lessons	d.	back bone
_____	5. achieve	e.	two times
_____	6. hurt	f.	mountains
_____	7. spine	g.	opportunity
_____	8. slopes	h.	classes
_____	9. training	i.	accomplish

SELECTION 2

BUILDING VOCABULARY SKILLS

SYNONYMS AND ANTONYMS

Decide if the following pairs of words are synonyms or antonyms. If they are synonyms, circle *S*. If they are antonyms, circle *A*.

1. flat   mountainous   S   A
2. evidence   proof   S   A
3. affect   influence   S   A
4. destroy   ruin   S   A
5. typical   usual   S   A
6. specific   general   S   A
7. powerless   powerful   S   A

EXPANDING VOCABULARY

Complete the following paragraph with words from the list.

limbs	disabled	hearing
programs	chance	injured
seeing	opportunity	

Many of the ski resorts in the United States have special _____ for _____ people. Some of the skiers have _____ their spines. Others have lost _____. Still others have problems _____ or _____. These programs provide an _____ for disabled people to do something exciting. It also gives them a _____ to face new challenges.

TALK IT OVER

DISCUSSION

1. What kind of challenges did Mike Utley face?

2. Mike Utley said, "Football was everything to me. I began playing when I was 7 years old. Now Vail has given me a chance to do something else." What do you think he meant by this statement? Discuss your ideas with your classmates.

3. Gwen Allard directs the program for disabled skiers at a resort in New York. She thinks that there is an important place in society for this type of program. Do you agree with her idea? If so, why do you think programs like the ones mentioned in the article are important?

SELECTION 3

FACING CHALLENGES / UNIT 3

Desak Made Suarti Laksmi is from Bali. She is a musician, composer, and dancer. She is best known for her talent in playing the gamelan, the traditional musical instruments of Bali. There are many kinds of gamelan instruments including drums, gongs, and xylophones. A gamelan orchestra usually plays for traditional occasions and ceremonies when there is dancing. The gamelan ensemble traditionally consists of at least twenty male musicians.

It is very unusual for a woman to play the gamelan. In **Sounds of Bali**, you will learn how and why Desak entered the male world of the gamelan, opening the door for other women.

BEFORE YOU READ

PREREADING DISCUSSION

1. Are there certain activities in your culture that are traditionally done only by men? Are there any that are traditionally done only by women? What are they? Make a list of examples and compare it with those of your classmates.

MEN	WOMEN
_____	_____
_____	_____
_____	_____
_____	_____

2. Are any of these traditional roles changing in your country? For example, are more women participating in traditionally male activities today?

_____
_____
_____
_____
_____
_____

Sounds of Bali

How long have you been playing the gamelan?

1   For almost my whole life. My father was a musician and dancer. He played the gamelan. I liked the sounds of the gamelan and began to teach myself to play when I was a very young child. By the time I was ten years old, I was teaching dance and gamelan to children in my family. Sometimes I played with my father.

Did your father encourage you to play the gamelan even though it was only played by men at that time?

2   Oh, yes. He knew I liked it so much and that I was very good at it. Everyone thought that it was very unusual to encourage a girl to play the gamelan. But I had a special talent for it, so he urged me to pursue it.

How would you describe gamelan music?

3   We do not play the gamelan from notes that are written down. We learn the songs by ear, according to how they sound. Each gamelan player's part in a song is different. When we play the gamelan, we have to pay attention to the sounds everyone else is making. The goal is beautiful, rhythmic sounds. Since all players have to connect to make the music beautiful, we must practice together a lot.

Did you have formal gamelan lessons?

4   Yes, I did. I was also a dancer. I went to the dance and music conservatory for high school. Before I graduated, I became a teacher there also. I went to STSI, the national college of the arts, after

high school. When I was there, I began to compose traditional and popular Balinese songs for the gamelan and for the voice. I was also a judge for gamelan contests.

5   After I graduated from college, I became a teacher at STSI. I taught singing, dancing, composing, and gamelan. I have traveled all over Bali teaching gamelan and judging competitions. My husband and I and our twin sons are now in the United States for three years. We are giving workshops and performances on Balinese theater, singing, dancing, and the gamelan. My husband is the assistant director of STSI and a master of Balinese masked theater.

Are more women learning the gamelan now in Bali because of your success?

6   Well, yes. Now there are some special competitions just for women. But you know, in Bali, the arts are important in everyone's daily life. We have ceremonies for birth, birthdays, marriage, death, and many other natural events. We have many, many ceremonies and festivals, and they always include a lot of singing, dancing, and music.

BUILDING READING SKILLS

ORGANIZING INFORMATION

Here is a list of some important events in Desak's life. Put them in the correct time order by numbering them from 1 to 6.

_____ began to compose traditional and popular Balinese songs for the gamelan

_____ taught herself to play the gamelan

_____ came to the United States to give workshops and performances on Balinese performing arts

_____ became a teacher at the national college of the arts

_____ began teaching dance and the gamelan to children in her family

_____ went to the dance and music conservatory for high school

SELECTION 3

HOW WELL DID YOU READ?

According to Desak, which of the following statements are true? Put a check mark on the line in front of the true statements.

_____ 1. In traditional Balinese society, both men and women played the gamelan.

_____ 2. Bali has a national college of the arts.

_____ 3. The goal of gamelan music is beautiful, rhythmic sounds.

_____ 4. The gamelan is usually played from music that is written down.

_____ 5. The arts are important in the daily lives of the Balinese people.

_____ 6. Music is an important part of the many ceremonies and festivals in Bali.

THINKING ABOUT THE INTERVIEW

What kind of challenges did Desak face?

_____

_____

BUILDING VOCABULARY SKILLS

PREFIXES

A prefix is a group of letters added to the beginning of a word to change its meaning. The prefix *un-* is often added to a word to mean *not*. For example, *unnecessary* means *not necessary*, and *unlucky* means *not lucky*.

The word *unusual* appears in the interview you have just read. "Everyone thought that it was very <u>unusual</u> to encourage a girl to play the gamelan." What do you think *unusual* means? _____

Read the following list of words that begin with the prefix *un-*. Then use the appropriate word to complete each of the sentences.

unknown   unbelievable   uncomfortable   uncertain   unclear

1. That sentence doesn't make sense. It's _____.

2. I don't have a map, and I'm _____ how to get to your house.

3. That story is amazing. In fact, it's _____.

4. The author of the book is _____.

5. My new skates were so _____ that I had to take them off.

Japan has the highest life expectancy rate for both men (75.9 years) and women (81.8 years).

SELECTION 4

FACING CHALLENGES / **UNIT 3**

Langston Hughes was an African-American author and poet. He was born in 1902 in Joplin, Missouri, and died in 1976. **Dreams** is one of his best-known poems. Listen as your teacher reads the poem to you. Then, read it to yourself several times.

ROUSSEAU, Henri. *The Sleeping Gypsy.* 1897.

Dreams

LANGSTON HUGHES

Hold fast to dreams
For when dreams die
Life is a broken-winged bird
That cannot fly.

Hold fast to dreams
For when dreams go
Life is a barren field
Frozen with snow.

THINKING ABOUT THE POEM

1. What two images does Langston Hughes use to describe lost dreams?

   _____   _____

2. Why do you think he chose these two images?

   _____

   _____

3. How do you think Langston Hughes would finish the sentence below?

   Dreams are very important: When you lose them, _____

   _____.

(continued on the next page)

71

SELECTION 4

4. The author Anaïs Nin once said, "Dreams are necessary to life."[1] Do you think Langston Hughes would agree with her? Why? Based on your own experience, how is this true? Do you think that setting goals is necessary to life?

5. Another American poet, William Burroughs, said, "There couldn't be a society of people who didn't dream. They'd be dead in two weeks."[2] What do you think he meant by that statement? Do you agree with this idea?

6. Jesse Jackson is an African-American clergyman and civil rights leader. He said, "We've removed the ceiling above our dreams. There are no more impossible dreams."[3] Do you agree with his statement? How do you think Langston Hughes would react to Jackson's idea? Do you think that there are any impossible goals? What about challenges that are too difficult to face?

[1] *The Diary of Anaïs Nin,* Vol. 1. June, 1933.
[2] Quoted in Victor Bockris, *With William Burroughs: A Report from the Bunker,* "On Dreams," 1981.
[3] *Independent,* London, June 9, 1988.

TYING IT ALL TOGETHER

FACING CHALLENGES / **UNIT 3**

JUST FOR FUN

CROSSWORD PUZZLE

Complete the crossword puzzle with words from the unit. Then check your answers in the Answer Key on page 209.

Across
1. Arms and legs
2. Backbone
5. Where you go to take classes
8. Orchestra in Bali
9. One of the instruments played in Bali
11. Small rivers
13. The opposite of *exactly*
17. A purpose
18. Yoko ____
19. Something skiers and runners participate in
20. A nickel is a ____.
21. Many people like to ____ songs.
22. A person who writes music
23. Home of the first marathon

Down
1. A famous African-American poet
2. Abbreviation for steam ship
3. The side of a mountain
4. A word that means *to urge*
6. When you take a risk, you take a ____ .
7. Many resorts have programs for disabled ____ .
10. We all have to face ____ .
11. Something you can do in winter
12. The statue of Johnny Kelley was made in his ____ .
14. A synonym for *evidence*
15. A twenty-six-mile race
16. Another word for *classes*

TYING IT ALL TOGETHER

DISCUSSION

1. An old proverb tells us, "If at first you don't succeed, try, try again." What does this mean? Why is this good advice?

2. Is there anyone in your life who had to overcome great difficulties in order to succeed? Spend a few minutes thinking about that person. What kind of difficulties did he or she overcome? Has this person been an inspiration to you? If so, how?

VOCABULARY REVIEW
WORK TOGETHER

In small groups, discuss the meaning of each of the following words from this unit. Write a definition or a synonym for each word. Try not to use your dictionary. Then, as a group, write a sentence for each word that shows you understand the meaning of the word. Share your sentences with the rest of the class.

1. chance _____
_____

2. twice _____
_____

3. limbs _____
_____

4. achieve _____
_____

5. injured _____
_____

6. training _____
_____

7. goal _____
_____

8. encourage _____
_____

9. tradition _____
_____

10. competition _____
_____

11. ceremony _____
_____

12. approximately _____
_____

13. unpredictable _____
_____

14. outstanding _____
_____

TYING IT ALL TOGETHER

SELF-TEST Complete the sentences with words from the list.

chance	limbs	twice
achieve	injured	training
goal	encouraged	tradition
competition	approximately	unpredictable
outstanding	ceremony	

1. John's poem won first prize in the poetry _____.

2. Desak's father _____ her to play the gamelan.

3. We have two arms and two legs. We have four _____.

4. It is difficult to learn to fly an airplane. Pilots need a lot of _____.

5. I'm not sure exactly how many students attend my university. There are _____ 5,000.

6. The weather at this time of year is _____. Some days, it is sunny and warm. Other days, it is cool and rainy.

7. If you try very hard, you can _____ your goals.

8. Pedro applied for a scholarship. He is a good student, and he has a good _____ of winning it.

9. Rachel got an A in every course this year. Her grades were _____.

10. Joyce fell _____ during the ski race. The first time nothing happened, but the second time she _____ her right knee.

11. In our family we always have dinner on Sundays at a special restaurant with our grandparents. It's a family _____.

12. David trains very hard every day. His _____ is to be in the Olympics.

13. Debbie and Don had a beautiful wedding _____.

FACING CHALLENGES / **UNIT 3**

READER'S JOURNAL

Think about the people and ideas you have read about and discussed in this unit. Choose a topic and write about it for ten to twenty minutes. You may pick a topic from the following list or choose one of your own.

- a challenge you have faced in the past
- something that interested you from one of the readings
- someone who has inspired you
- a goal you have set for yourself
- your own poem called "Dreams"
- your thoughts on one of the questions from the Points to Ponder or Tying It All Together sections

READER'S JOURNAL

Date: _____

BRAIN-POWER

Selections

1. Do You Know Your Right Brain from Your Left? . .81
2. Albert Einstein:
   The Man and the Legends about Him 86
3. How Good Is Your Memory? 92

"The brain is in a class by itself. Compared with other organs in the body, it has complexity and beauty." Herbert Lourie, M.D.

The human mind is very powerful. As you work through this unit, you will learn about your own mind and the amazing ways the human mind works. You will also learn something about the special mind of Albert Einstein.

POINTS TO PONDER

Answer each of the following questions about yourself. Then discuss your answers with your classmates in small groups.

1. What types of things are you good at? Make a list.

   _____
   _____
   _____
   _____

2. What types of things do you find difficult or challenging? Make a list.

   _____
   _____
   _____
   _____

When he was twenty-six years old, Gon Yang-ling of Harbin, China, memorized more than 15,000 telephone numbers.

3. Do you have a good memory? Are you good at memorizing certain things? What types of things are you best at memorizing or remembering? Do you use any "tricks" to help you remember things? What are they?

4. Is your mind most active during the morning, during the afternoon, during the evening, or at night? Are you more creative when you are asleep or awake?

SELECTION 1

BRAINPOWER / **UNIT 4**

We all use both sides of our brains, but some of us favor one side over the other. The side we favor is called the dominant side. Knowing which side you favor can help you understand a lot about yourself. **Do You Know Your Right Brain from Your Left?** will explore the two sides of the brain—the right and the left.

BEFORE YOU READ
PREREADING ACTIVITY

To see if you have a dominant side, read sections A and B in the quiz below. Then put a check mark next to the statements that are true for you. Be honest!

Are You Right-Brained or Left-Brained?

A

B

1. I'm good at math. ____

2. I keep a to-do list. ____

3. If I have to assemble something, I read the instructions first. ____

4. I feel comfortable expressing myself with words. ____

5. Before I make a decision on an issue, I like to get all the facts first. ____

6. I always wear a watch. ____

1. When I talk, I use my hands a lot. ____

2. I like to draw. ____

3. When I'm confused, I usually use my instincts. ____

4. I lose track of time easily. ____

5. I think it is boring to follow a schedule. ____

6. I am a musical person. ____

(continued on the next page)

SELECTION 1

7. If I forget someone's name, I go through the alphabet until I remember it. ____
8. I have thought about being a lawyer, a journalist, or a doctor. ____
9. I'd make a good detective. ____
10. I believe there is a right and a wrong way to do everything. ____
11. I like to set goals for myself. ____
12. If I have a difficult decision to make, I write down the pros and cons. ____
13. I keep a journal. ____
14. If someone asks me a question, I usually turn my head to the right. ____
15. If I lose something, I try to remember where I saw it last. ____
16. The expression "Life is just a bowl of cherries"[1] makes no sense to me. ____

TOTAL _____

7. I can tell if people are guilty just by looking at them. ____
8. I've thought about being a poet, a politician, an architect, or a dancer. ____
9. I believe there are two sides to every story. ____
10. I'd rather draw a map than tell someone how to get somewhere. ____
11. If I have a problem, I try to solve it by relating it to a similar problem I've had in the past. ____
12. When someone asks me a question, I turn my head to the left. ____
13. If I don't know what to do, I follow my emotions. ____
14. Some people think I'm psychic.[2] ____
15. I'm often late getting places. ____
16. I hate following directions. ____

TOTAL _____

> SCORING: Add up the number of check marks in columns A and B. If your total for column A is higher, you rely more on your left brain. If your total in column B is higher, you rely more on your right brain. If your totals are the same, or are very close, you probably use both sides of your brain equally.

[1] **life is just a bowl of cherries** Life is wonderful.
[2] **psychic** Someone who has special mental powers such as the ability to predict the future.

BRAINPOWER / UNIT 4

Do You Know Your Right Brain from Your Left?

1. The human brain is divided into two sides, or hemispheres, called the right brain and the left brain. The two hemispheres work together, but each one specializes in certain ways of thinking. Each side has its own way of using information to help us think, understand, and process information.

2. The left side of the brain controls language. It is more verbal and logical. It names things and puts them into groups. It uses rules and likes ideas to be clear, logical, and orderly. It is best at speech, reading, writing, and math. You use this side of the brain when you memorize spelling and grammar rules or when you do a math problem.

3. The right side of the brain is more visual and creative. It specializes in using information it receives from the senses of sight, sound, smell, touch, and taste. This side of the brain likes to dream and experiment. It controls your appreciation of music, color, and art. You use this side when you draw a picture or listen to music.

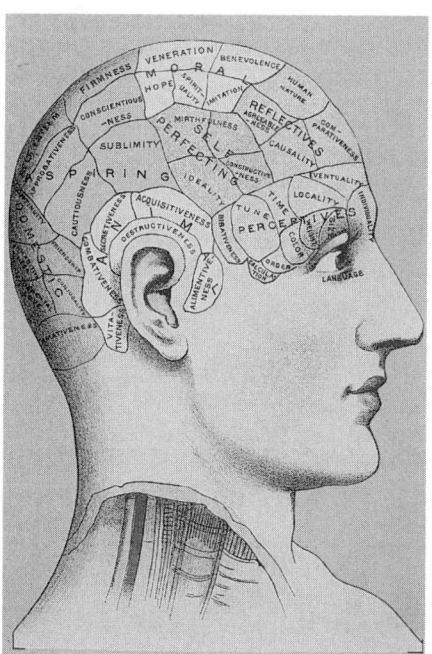

4. Although we all use both sides of our brains, one side is usually stronger or dominant. Some people are more "left-brained," and others are more "right-brained." Our dominant side influences the kinds of jobs and hobbies we have. Politicians, artists, architects, and musicians depend on their right brains. Accountants, engineers, doctors, and lawyers usually rely on their left brains.

SELECTION 1

BUILDING READING SKILLS
IDENTIFYING MAIN IDEAS

Which of the following topics are discussed in the article? Put a check mark next to those topics.

_____ 1. the side of the brain that is more logical

_____ 2. the size and weight of the human brain

_____ 3. the side of the brain that is more creative

_____ 4. the types of people that are usually right-brained or left-brained

_____ 5. the part of the brain that controls muscular activity

_____ 6. diseases of the brain

BUILDING READING SKILLS
LOCATING MAIN IDEAS

Answer the following questions by writing the number of the paragraph on the lines provided.

1. Which paragraph describes the left brain? (¶_____)

2. Which paragraph explains that the human brain is divided into two sides? (¶_____)

3. Which paragraph discusses the kind of people who are usually left-brained or right-brained? (¶_____)

4. Which paragraph describes the right brain? (¶_____)

HOW WELL DID YOU READ?

Read the following statements. If a statement is true, write *T* on the line provided. If it is false, write *F*.

_____ 1. The human brain has two sides.

_____ 2. Everyone is more right-brained than left-brained.

_____ 3. The right side of the brain is more creative.

_____ 4. When you solve a math problem, you use your left brain.

_____ 5. Both sides of the brain specialize in the same things.

_____ 6. Artists use their right brain more than engineers do.

_____ 7. When you paint a picture, you use your left brain.

APPLICATION OF INFORMATION

Read the following descriptions of four different people. Decide who you think is left-brained and who is right-brained. Write *Left* next to the descriptions of left-brained people and *Right* next to the descriptions of right-brained people.

_____ 1. Daniel's hobby is drawing cartoons. He loves surprises and hates following a strict schedule. He is very sensitive and likes to find new ways of doing things.

_____ 2. Dr. Curley is very careful about keeping his appointments. He is always on time and does things in an orderly way. Every day, as soon as he gets home from work, he takes his dog for a walk and goes jogging for a half hour.

_____ 3. Debbie is a lawyer at a big law firm in New York. Her language skills are very good. She is a very logical person. She gets up, eats, and goes to sleep at the same time every day.

_____ 4. Ian Baker is the mayor of a small city. He is always looking for creative ways to solve the city's problems. In his spare time, he enjoys going to concerts and playing the piano.

EXPANDING VOCABULARY

Complete each sentence with a word from the list.

hemispheres	specializes	information	verbal
rules	memorize	logical	creative
dominant			

1. Artists are _____ people.

2. Our brains have two _____.

3. The left side of an accountant's brain is probably _____.

4. English spelling _____ are very complicated.

5. _____ people have good language skills.

6. Each side of the brain uses _____ in a different way.

7. The right side of the brain _____ in using knowledge it gets from the senses.

8. The lawyer gave a _____ argument. It made sense.

9. It is difficult to _____ all the English grammar rules.

FYI

Cats can catch rabbits even though rabbits are faster. This is because cats are smarter than rabbits. They have a better brain.

SELECTION 2

Albert Einstein is one of the most famous scientists of the twentieth century. He was born in 1879 in Germany and became a U.S. citizen in 1940. Einstein received the Nobel Prize in physics in 1921. His theories have changed the way we think about the universe and the dimensions of time and space. Read the following article, **Albert Einstein: The Man and the Legends about Him**, to learn more about the life of this great man.

BEFORE YOU READ

PREREADING DISCUSSION

1. Write the first five words that come into your mind when you think of the word *genius*.

   _____

   _____

   _____

   _____

   _____

   Compare your list with your classmates' lists.

2. Have you ever known someone whom you think is a genius? In what area? How would you describe this person? What qualities did he or she have that were special?

Albert Einstein: The Man and the Legends about Him

1. Albert Einstein's early childhood would not lead anyone to predict that he would become the most famous and influential physicist of his time. He did not talk at all until the age of three, late in almost any culture. One "legend" has it that young Albert finally broke his silence at the supper table one night saying, "The soup is too hot." His parents asked why he had never said a word until then, and Albert replied, "Because up to now everything was alright."

2. Einstein was born in Ulm, Württemberg, Germany in 1879. He disliked his early years in school and studied primarily at home. His limitless curiosity showed up in questions like, "Why does a compass needle always point in the same direction?" at the age of five, and, "What would the world look like if I rode on a beam of light?" at age 14. He never lost his curiosity. As an adult he said, "The most beautiful thing we can experience is the mysterious. It is the source of all true art and science."

3. In 1905, Einstein published four papers which revolutionized modern physics. In 1915, he published his general theory of relativity. His famous equation $E = mc^2$ (energy equals mass times the velocity of light squared) is a cornerstone of the modern nuclear age. And he won the Nobel prize for physics in 1921.

4. Einstein was of Jewish descent, and in 1933 the Nazi government of Germany took away his property and citizenship. He then moved to the United States.

SELECTION 2

5 Einstein became a member of the staff of the Institute for Advanced Studies in Princeton, New Jersey. In 1944, he became an American citizen. He lived a quiet personal life. He enjoyed classical music, and played the violin. After a session with a group of fellow musicians, one of them was reported to have said, "He'd be a good musician if only he could count!" An interesting comment to make about a man whose life work involved highly complex mathematical thinking.

6 Einstein kept his sense of humor throughout his life. A magazine called *Scientific American* once had a competition for the best explanation of the theory of relativity in three thousand words. Einstein said, "I'm the only one in my entire circle of friends who is not entering. I don't believe I could do it."

HOW WELL DID YOU READ?

Read the following statements. If a statement is true, write *T* on the line. If it is false, write *F*.

_____ 1. Einstein learned to talk at a very early age.

_____ 2. As a child, Einstein was very curious, and he continued to be curious throughout his life.

_____ 3. Einstein's theory of relativity revolutionized physics.

_____ 4. Einstein was born in Germany. He lived there his entire life.

_____ 5. Einstein had a good sense of humor.

_____ 6. He had a very active social life.

_____ 7. One of Einstein's hobbies was playing the violin.

_____ 8. Albert Einstein won the Nobel prize for physics.

BUILDING READING SKILLS
SCANNING FOR DETAILS

Read the following questions about Albert Einstein. Then scan the article to find the answers. Work as quickly as possible. Do not reread every word in the article. As soon as you find the answer to a question, move on to the next one.

1. Where was Einstein born? _____

2. When did he publish his papers about the theory of relativity? _____

3. What prize did he win in 1921? _____

4. What musical instrument did Einstein play? _____

5. When did he become an American citizen? _____

BUILDING VOCABULARY SKILLS
WORD FORMS

Complete each sentence with the correct word.

1. predict   predictions

   a. Can you _____ what this article will be about?

   b. Some people like to make _____ about the future.

2. mysterious   mystery

   a. No one could figure out how the fire started. It is a _____.

   b. I don't know Dr. Brown very well. But he seems like a

      _____ person.

3. curious   curiosity

   a. Einstein was _____ about the world around him.

   b. Have you ever heard the expression "_____ killed the cat, satisfaction brought it back"?

4. beauty   beautiful

   a. My French teacher is one of the most _____ women I have ever seen.

   b. Do you agree with the expression, "_____ is only skin deep"?

5. mathematical   math

   a. Einstein's work involved highly complex _____ concepts.

   b. Joe's favorite subject in school is _____.

6. competition   competes

   a. My brother _____ in the Boston Marathon every year.

   b. Eric entered a poem in the school poetry _____.

SELECTION 2

READ AND REACT

The following are some of Einstein's famous quotes. In small groups, discuss their meanings. Some of the words are difficult. Before you use your dictionary, see if someone in your group can explain unfamiliar words to you.

1. *Imagination is more important than knowledge.*

2. *It is the supreme art of the teacher to awaken joy in creative expression and knowledge.*

3. *Do not worry about your difficulties in mathematics. I can assure you that mine are still greater.*

4. *Great spirits have always encountered violent opposition from mediocre minds.*

5. *The whole of science is nothing more than a refinement of everyday thinking.*

BRAIN TEASERS

Test your skill at solving the following puzzles. Then check your answers in the Answer Key on page 209.

1. Two U.S. coins equal thirty cents. One is not a quarter. What are the two coins?

2. A man walked into a pet shop and bought a parrot. The parrot was guaranteed to repeat everything it heard. However, the parrot never said a word. Why not?

3. A plane crashed on the border of Canada and the United States. Where should they bury the survivors?

4. Suppose you are driving from Philadelphia to Boston at a speed of 90 miles per hour (mph). At the same time, your friend is driving from Boston to Philadelphia at a speed of 60 mph. When the two cars meet, who is closer to Boston?

5. Two brothers were born on the same day, at the same time, in the same year, and at the same hospital. They have the same mother and father, but they are not twins. What are they?

6. A ship has a ladder on one side. There are 25 cm between each step. Ten steps of the ladder are under water at high tide and twenty steps are above water. If the water level goes down 75 cm at low tide, how many steps will be outside the water?

7. A spider is at the bottom of a thirty-meter hole. The spider is trying to climb out. It climbs up four meters in daylight, but at night it becomes confused and climbs down three meters. At this rate, how long will it take the spider to crawl out?

8. John, Carol, Steve, Tom, Mary, and David all like music. Two of the people are teachers and the other four are students. The teachers give lessons in two of the following instruments: tuba, saxophone, guitar, or drums. The students each take lessons in one of those instruments. Use the clues below to answer the following questions:

   a. Who are the teachers? _____ _____

   b. Which two instruments do they teach? _____
   _____

   c. Who are the students? _____ _____
   _____ _____

   d. Which instrument is each one learning? _____
   _____ _____ _____

   CLUES:
   - The drum student is not a woman.
   - Carol has never played a brass instrument.
   - Mary has never met Tom.
   - Steve often helps the saxophone teacher give lessons.
   - The tuba teacher told her student to practice more.
   - John is the saxophone student.
   - Steve is a teacher.

SELECTION 3

How Good Is Your Memory? is an interview with a teacher and psychotherapist, Diane Englund. Through her work, Ms. Englund has learned that different people gather and remember information in different ways. This observation has led her to an interest in how the brain processes and remembers information.

BEFORE YOU READ
PREREADING ACTIVITY

Before you read the following interview about memory, think about the types of things that are easy or difficult for you to remember. Put *E* next to the items below that are easy for you to remember. Put *D* next to the ones that are difficult for you to remember.

_____ names
_____ words to songs
_____ math formulas
_____ faces
_____ phone numbers
_____ addresses

_____ speeches
_____ sports statistics
_____ directions
_____ birthdays
_____ historical facts

● ●

How Good Is Your Memory?

What aspects of brain biology interest you?

1 I have become very interested in the importance of memory in our lives. Most people know that the brain controls how the body works. The brain also controls what the mind thinks, how we feel, how we process information, and how we perceive things. I am interested in how people remember, what they remember, and how they use and improve their memories.

What can you tell us about memory?

2 Memory plays an important role in learning and thinking. People have different abilities to remember. Stress, fatigue, emotional problems, and illness can decrease the ability to remember. General good health contributes to good memory. Practice also improves memory. For example, the more math facts you learn, the easier math facts are to learn. The same is true with music. The more songs you listen to and learn, the easier it becomes. People gather and remember information in different ways. Some people remember colors or smells or sounds. Other people find it easier to remember spoken words. While still others remember printed words easily.

Are there different kinds of memory?

3 Yes. The two basic categories are long-term memory and short-term memory. Long-term memory is the ability to remember events from the distant past. Long-term memory is often the strongest and lasts throughout a person's life. One kind of long-term memory is called "screen memory." This means that many experiences get put together in the mind as one memory. For example, in your memory you might have only one "picture" of a childhood trip to the doctor's office. This one memory, however, is probably a combination of many trips to the doctor.

4 Short-term memory is the ability to remember events in the recent past, for example the name of someone you met at a party last night. Short-term memory is often challenged by stress, illness, and aging. Many of us have, or have had, grandparents who remember events from their childhood with great accuracy, but are unable to remember what happened yesterday. Most people can only remember seven items in sequence. This is why telephone numbers, for example, are typically seven digits long.

Are all memories accurate?

5 No, not all memories are correct, but they all tell us something about the person who is doing the remembering. The memory may tell us what the rememberer likes or dislikes, what he or she wishes, and it may also tell us about his or her fears. The study of memory may also provide information about the health or illness of a person. This is a very exciting frontier in biological science. There is still a lot for us to learn.

SELECTION 3

Why is it easier for people to remember some things and more difficult for them to remember other things.

6   That's a good question. It's easier to remember things that have emotional meaning to you. It's also easier to remember information that you practice and use a lot. Repetition reinforces memory; the more you repeat something, the better you remember it. Some people have very visual memories. That is, they remember things they see. In fact, it is often easier to remember information that comes to us through more than one of our five senses.

HOW WELL DID YOU READ?

Read the following statements. If a statement is true, write *T* on the line. If it is false, write *F*.

_____ 1. The state of your health can affect your ability to remember things accurately.

_____ 2. All people gather and remember information in the same way.

_____ 3. The two basic kinds of memory are long-term memory and screen memory.

_____ 4. Short-term memory is the ability to remember things in the recent past.

_____ 5. Scientists have already discovered almost everything there is to know about memory.

_____ 6. The brain controls not only the way the body works but also the way the mind thinks.

_____ 7. We can learn many things by examining what a person remembers.

EXPANDING VOCABULARY

Cross out the word in each group that does not belong.

1. stress   fatigue   illness   practice
2. think   jump   feel   perceive
3. kinds   categories   trips   groups
4. sequence   order   memory   series
5. typically   usually   generally   rarely
6. correct   wrong   accurate   true

BRAINPOWER / **UNIT 4**

USING EXAMPLES

Authors often use examples to support their ideas. In her interview, Ms. Englund used several examples to support her ideas and make them easier to understand. Look back through the interview and find the examples she used to support the following points.

1. Screen memory is a combination of many experiences that get put together in the mind as one memory.

   _____
   _____

2. Most people can only remember seven items in sequence.

   _____
   _____

3. Practice improves memory.

   _____
   _____

The brain of an average adult male weighs 3 pounds 2.2 ounces (1.42 kilograms). The average woman's brain weighs 2 pounds 6 ounces (1.08 kilograms). There is no correlation between brain weight and intelligence.

95

TYING IT ALL TOGETHER

DISCUSSION

1. Swiss philosopher Henri-Frédéric Amiel once said, "To do easily what is difficult for others is the mark of talent. To do what is impossible for talented people is the mark of genius." What do you think he meant? Do you agree with him?

2. Most people think it's wonderful to have a good memory, but there may be some things you wish you could forget. Alexander Durivage, author and historian, stated this idea very well when he said, "They teach us to remember; why don't they teach us to forget? Memory can be a curse as well as a blessing." Discuss this quote with your classmates. Do you have some memories you wish you could forget?

3. Thomas Edison is famous for inventing the electric light bulb and the phonograph.[1] He believed, "Genius is one percent inspiration and 99 percent perspiration." What do you think?

JUST FOR FUN
BRAIN TEASER

Try this brain teaser on some friends and see how many answer, "A gray elephant from Denmark."

1. Choose a number from 2 to 9, but don't say it out loud.

2. Multiply that number by 9.

3. Add the 2 digits of your answer together.

4. Subtract 5 from the answer.

5. Choose the letter of the English alphabet that your answer corresponds to. For example, 1 is A, 2 is B, and so on.

6. Think of a country that starts with that letter.

7. Take the second letter of the name of that country, and think of the biggest animal that starts with that letter.

8. Think of the color of that animal.

9. Ask, "Is your answer a gray elephant from Denmark?"

Can you figure out why most people end up with this answer?

---

[1] **phonograph** A record player.

BRAINPOWER / **UNIT 4**

PERSPECTIVE DRAWING

Look at the drawing. Don't let your brain play tricks on you. At first glance the drawing looks fine. But when you look at it more closely, you will realize that much of the drawing does not make sense. Identify and describe as many of the mistakes as you can. Then check your answers in the Answer Key on page 210.

97

TYING IT ALL TOGETHER

VOCABULARY REVIEW

WORK TOGETHER

In small groups, discuss the meaning of each of the following words from this unit. Write a definition or a synonym for each word. Try not to use your dictionary. Then, as a group, write a sentence for each word that shows you understand the meaning of the word. Share your sentences with the rest of the class.

1. compete _____

2. predict _____

3. logical _____

4. perceive _____

5. combination _____

6. verbal _____

7. entire _____

8. accurate _____

9. contribute _____

10. memorize _____

11. mystery _____

12. specialize _____

13. creative _____

14. curious _____

15. sequence _____

SELF-TEST

Complete the sentences with words from the list.

specializes   compete
logical   predicts
sequence   entire
accurate   creative
mystery   memorize
curious   combination
verbal   perceive
contribute

1. The cause of the fire is still a _____. No one knows how it started.

2. The radio station plays a _____ of classical music, rock and roll, and jazz.

3. Harvey is a doctor. He _____ in problems of the heart.

4. Juliette is a very _____ child. Although she is only two years old, she already speaks in complete sentences.

(continued on the next page)

TYING IT ALL TOGETHER

5. Not many people can read an _____ book in one day.

6. Some people find it difficult to _____ speeches. They prefer to refer to their notes.

7. The police are trying to discover the _____ of events that happened on the night of the murder.

8. Every four years, soccer teams from around the world _____ for the World Cup.

9. When I looked at the twins, I couldn't _____ any difference between them. They looked exactly the same to me. However, their parents can tell them apart easily.

10. Judy received a package in the mail. She was so _____ about what was inside that she opened it up immediately.

11. Eating well and getting exercise _____ to good health.

12. The weatherman says it won't be a good day for a picnic. He _____ that it will rain.

13. This clock never tells the correct time. It's not very _____.

14. Jim is a musician. He also likes to paint and write poetry. All his friends think he is a very _____ person.

15. Matt is left-brained. He is a mathematician and his thinking is always very _____.

READER'S JOURNAL

Think about the topics that you have read about and discussed in this unit. Choose a topic and write about it for ten to twenty minutes. You may pick a topic from the following list, or you may choose one of your own. Or you could write your reaction to one of the quotations you read in this unit.

- how to improve your memory
- your definition of a genius
- the differences between right-brained and left-brained people
- Are you right-brained or left-brained?
- your thoughts on one of the questions from the Points to Ponder or Tying It All Together Sections

READER'S JOURNAL

Date: _____

CLIMATE CONTROL

Unit·5

Selections

1. Winter Blues, Summer Blahs 105
2. Climate: A Powerful Force 109
3. What's the Weather? 117

Climate controls our lives more than most of us realize. In this unit, you will read about some of the unusual ways that the weather and climate have affected human life.

POINTS TO PONDER

Answer each of the following questions about yourself. Then discuss your answers in small groups.

1. How are you affected by the weather? Make a list of the ways.

   _____

   _____

   _____

   _____

2. What is your favorite climate?

3. Do you prefer hot weather or cold weather? Why? Which do you like better, winter sports or summer sports?

Winter sports: skating   Summer sports: surfing

SELECTION 1

CLIMATE CONTROL / **UNIT 5**

Many people are affected by changes in temperature or weather. Are you one of these people? Answer the following questions and then read **Winter Blues, Summer Blahs**.

BEFORE YOU READ

PREREADING ACTIVITY

Think about the ways seasons affect you and circle your answers to the questions. Then discuss your answers with classmates.

When the seasons change . . .		
1. Do you find you have less energy than usual?	Yes	No
2. Do you feel less creative or productive?	Yes	No
3. Do you feel sad, down, or depressed?	Yes	No
4. Do you feel less enthusiastic about the future or enjoy your life less?	Yes	No
5. Do you need more sleep than usual?	Yes	No
6. Do you feel you have no control over your appetite or weight?	Yes	No

Winter Blues, Summer Blahs

[1] The weather affects all of us in some way. Some of us, however, are especially sensitive to changes in the weather. For several years, psychiatrists have been studying groups of people who become depressed when the seasons change. These people suffer from a condition called Seasonal Affective Disorder (SAD). Some people have a very mild form,

which does not disrupt their lives too much. Other people have a severe form, and they are not able to function well when the seasons change.

2   Millions of people have SAD in some form. It affects about four times as many women as men, usually adults between the ages of twenty and forty years old. However, even school children can be affected by SAD. There are more cases of SAD among people who live in countries with colder climates.

3   The most common form of SAD occurs in winter, when the days get shorter. The reason is that there is not as much bright sunlight in the winter. Changes in seasons and weather cause chemical reactions in the brain that can affect our behavior and moods. The way we feel, how much we eat and sleep, and how well we deal with stress can all be affected by changes in the weather. For example, in the winter, some people complain of being tired all the time and having less interest in socializing. Others tend to overeat and gain weight. Difficulty with concentration and work are also typical symptoms of winter seasonal disorder. People with mild winter blues probably don't need medical treatment. A long walk in the middle of the day usually helps and so do bright lights in the home and office. Special fluorescent lights that provide artificial sunlight can be purchased and are also helpful. When spring comes, most SAD sufferers feel fine again.

4   Although it is less common, some people suffer from summer seasonal disorder. It is thought that intense heat and humidity cause the problems. Symptoms include nervousness, agitation, sleeplessness, loss of appetite and weight, and a lack of energy. There are not many ways to treat summer depression except for staying in air-conditioning.

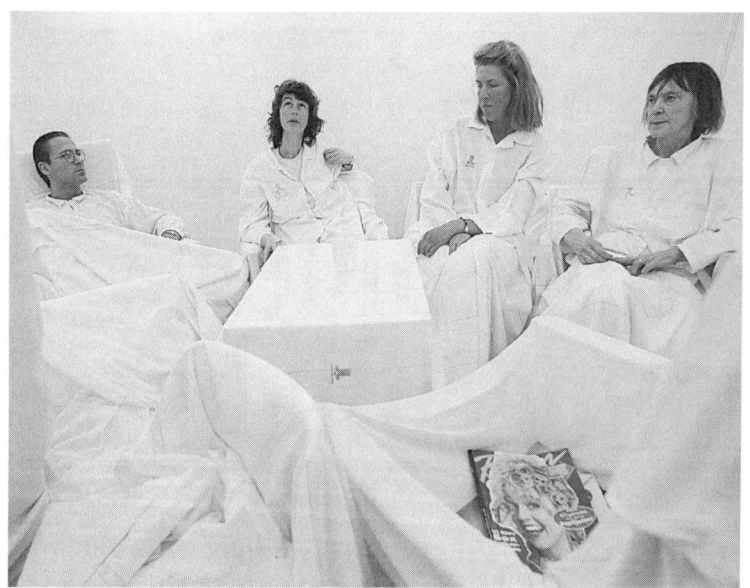

Hospital patients in Stockholm, Sweden, sit in artificial sun for two hours a day to fight depression from light deprivation in winter.

CLIMATE CONTROL / **UNIT 5**

BUILDING READING SKILLS

IDENTIFYING MAIN IDEAS

Which of the following topics are discussed in the article? Put a check mark next to those topics.

_____ 1. the kinds of people who are usually affected by SAD

_____ 2. the symptoms and effects of SAD

_____ 3. an explanation of the medical treatments for SAD

_____ 4. the causes of SAD

_____ 5. the ways teachers can help children who have SAD

_____ 6. the types of SAD

HOW WELL DID YOU READ?

Read each of the following statements. If a statement is true, write *T* on the line. If it is false, write *F*.

_____ 1. SAD affects more women than men.

_____ 2. Some people have a mild form of SAD, while others have a more severe form.

_____ 3. The most common form of SAD occurs in the summer, when the days are longer.

_____ 4. Changes in the weather can affect our behavior.

_____ 5. Medical treatment is always necessary for people who suffer from SAD.

_____ 6. The lack of bright sunlight is an important cause of SAD.

_____ 7. Children are never affected by SAD.

_____ 8. The symptoms of SAD are the same for everyone who suffers from it.

BUILDING VOCABULARY SKILLS

SYNONYMS AND ANTONYMS

Decide if the following pairs of words are synonyms or antonyms. If they are synonyms, circle *S*. If they are antonyms, circle *A*.

1. mild   severe   S   A

2. purchase   buy   S   A

3. intense   strong   S   A

(continued on the next page)

SELECTION 1

4. depressed	sad	S	A
5. shorter	longer	S	A
6. gain	loss	S	A

EXPANDING VOCABULARY

Complete each sentence with a word from the list.

suffer	sensitive	affect	treat
behavior	symptoms	seasons	function

1. Some people are more _____ to changes in the weather than others.

2. More people _____ from SAD in the winter than in the summer.

3. Loss of appetite and lack of energy are some of the _____ of summer SAD.

4. Many people are not able to _____ well when the _____ change.

5. A walk in the middle of the day is one way to _____ winter SAD.

6. Changes in our _____ and moods are common when the weather changes.

7. Do changes in the weather _____ you?

> **FYI**
>
> The South Pole gets no sunshine for 182 days per year. The North Pole gets no sunshine for 176 days. St. Petersburg, Florida, had 768 sunny days in a row between 1967 and 1969.

DISCUSSION

YOU WRITE THE QUESTIONS

In this activity, you will write the questions for class discussion. In small groups, write two discussion questions based on the article you have just read. Then exchange your questions with those of another group. Discuss the answers to the questions with the members of your group.

1. _____

_____

2. _____

_____

SELECTION 2

CLIMATE CONTROL / **UNIT 5**

Climate is a powerful force that affects many aspects of our lives. The types of houses we build, the kinds of clothes we wear, the food we eat, how we spend our free time, and even our countries' economic development are all influenced by climate. In **Climate: A Powerful Force,** you will read about the many ways that climate affects human life.

BEFORE YOU READ

PREREADING ACTIVITY

1. Make a list of all the words and phrases you can think of that have to do with weather and climate. Then compare your list with those of your classmates.

   _____ _____ _____

   _____ _____ _____

   _____ _____ _____

   _____ _____ _____

2. With a partner, discuss some of the ways that climate affects your life.

● ●

Climate: A Powerful Force

1   Most people probably spend more time thinking about weather than about climate. Although weather and climate are closely related, climate is different from weather. Weather refers to the temperature and amount of rain, wind, sun, and snow during a specific time. On the other hand, climate refers to the typical weather patterns of an area over many years. So, climate is a long view of weather.

2   Several natural factors determine the climate of an area. They include the amount of heat an area receives from the sun, the distance it is from the equator, whether the land is flat or mountainous, and how close it is to a body of water. For these reasons, places that are far away from each other may have similar climates and places that are close to each other may have different climates.

SELECTION 2

3   Few of us give much thought to the ways that climate has transformed human life over the course of history or to the ways that humans have learned to adapt to the changes in climate that have taken place. Climate is something that we typically take for granted, yet it is important to understand how it has shaped our behaviors over time.

4   Climates do not remain the same. They have changed dramatically many times throughout history. There have been several ice ages followed by periods of warming. In a meeting in Rio de Janeiro, scientists discussed the global climate of the future. They studied how climate has changed in the past and how these changes have transformed life on our planet. For hundreds of millions of years, powerful astronomical and geological forces have been at work causing the earth's environment to alternate between periods of hot and cold, and wet and dry. As climates warmed and cooled, plants and animals appeared and disappeared in the changing environment. Some scientists now believe that the drastic changes in our planet's climate have played a big part in human evolution.

5   Scientists have found evidence of these shifts in climate in every part of the world. For example, they have discovered evidence of subtropical plants north of the Arctic Circle. There is also evidence that 5,000 years ago the Sahara Desert had areas of green. They know that people have had to change their way of life many times as plant and animal life shifted over the world. There are even cases of ancient cities and cultures that were destroyed by changes in the amount of rainfall.

The Tuaregs—nomads of the Sahara Desert—wear turbans on their heads for protection against sandstorms and the sun.

6   Human life and climate are interrelated. Climate affects our behavior much more than we realize. It affects the kinds of clothes we wear and even the colors we choose to wear. Since it affects the kinds of crops we can grow successfully, it influences our eating habits. Architecture is also affected by climate. Engineers and architects must think about climate when they make decisions about the construction, materials, design, and style of buildings. Even our choices in transportation are determined by the climate in which we live. Climate also plays a big part in economic development. A climate that is too hot or too dry makes farming, industry, and transportation difficult and slows economic development down.

7   Climate has played a dominant role in human development, and much of recorded history tells how people

have dealt with their climate. In recent times, technological advances have helped us get some control over our environment. Heating and air conditioning, for example, have made it easier for us to adapt to climate.

8   Not only does climate affect human behavior, but human activity may also affect climate. By changing the earth's surface and introducing chemicals such as carbon dioxide into the atmosphere, humans may have had an impact on the climate. Since 1938, scientists have noticed an increased amount of CO_2 in the atmosphere. This increase could raise the temperature of the earth. Scientists worry that human activity such as burning coal, oil, and natural gas, for example, will cause a global change to a warmer climate. A warming of the atmosphere would have a huge effect on our environment. It would speed the melting of the ice caps and raise sea levels. This would change the climate and have a profound effect on plant and animal life.

9   We have learned a lot in our years on planet Earth. However, the question is, have we learned enough? Since we do not know the consequences of trying to control the weather, we cannot know what future problems we are causing when we try to manipulate our environment.

BUILDING READING SKILLS

IDENTIFYING MAIN IDEAS

Which of the following topics are discussed in the article? Put a check mark next to those topics.

_____ 1. the difference between weather and climate

_____ 2. the typical climate in North America

_____ 3. the effects of climate on our lives

_____ 4. natural factors that affect climate

_____ 5. a description of life during the ice ages

HOW WELL DID YOU READ?

Read the following statements. If a statement is true, write *T* on the line. If it is false, write *F*.

_____ 1. *Climate* and *weather* mean the same thing.

_____ 2. Climate affects human behavior.

(*continued on the next page*)

SELECTION 2

_____ 3. The climate of an area always stays the same.

_____ 4. An increase in the amount of CO_2 in the atmosphere lowers the temperature on earth.

_____ 5. We do not know how trying to control the weather will affect the future.

TALK IT OVER

DISCUSSION

1. Discuss the ways that each of the following statements from the article is true.

   a. Climate affects the kinds of clothes we wear.
   b. Climate affects the crops we grow and the foods we eat.
   c. Architecture is affected by climate.
   d. Transportation is determined by climate.

2. The author of the article said that heaters and air conditioners have made it easier for humans to adapt to climate. Do you agree with this idea? Or do you think that people who do not use heaters and air conditioners are better adapted?

BASIC READING SKILLS

SUPPORTING MAIN IDEAS

Find support for each of the following main ideas in the article. Refer to the article to complete the chart.

Main Idea	Support
Human life and climate are interrelated.	
Several natural factors affect climate.	
Climates do not remain the same.	

112

CLIMATE CONTROL / **UNIT 5**

EXPANDING VOCABULARY

A. Circle the letter of the word that is closest in meaning to the underlined word.

1. *Climates do not <u>remain</u> the same.*

    a. stay
    b. look
    c. control

2. *There are even cases of ancient cities and cultures that were <u>destroyed</u> by changes in the amount of rainfall.*

    a. built
    b. found
    c. ruined

3. *Some scientists now believe that the <u>drastic</u> changes in our planet's climate have played a big part in human evolution.*

    a. helpful
    b. extreme
    c. small

4. *Climate refers to the <u>typical</u> weather patterns of an area over many years.*

    a. usual
    b. different
    c. strange

The wettest inhabited place in the world is Buenaventura, Colombia, with an average annual rainfall of 265.47 inches (6,743 mm). The driest inhabited place is Aswan, Egypt, with 0.02 inches (0.5 mm) of rain annually.

5. *Since animal and plant life <u>vary</u> according to climate, scientists have been able to identify some of the shifts.*

    a. grow
    b. decide
    c. change

6. *We cannot know what future problems we are causing when we try to <u>manipulate</u> our environment.*

    a. predict
    b. control
    c. destroy

SELECTION 2

B. Matching. Match each word with its meaning. Write the correct letter on the line.

WORD	MEANING
_____ 1. climate	a. temperature, rain, wind, sun, snow during a specific time
_____ 2. crops	b. the covering with water of a place that is usually dry
_____ 3. drought	
_____ 4. weather	c. the work of building something
_____ 5. flood	d. usual behavior
_____ 6. construction	e. long period of dry weather
_____ 7. habits	f. plants grown for food
	g. typical weather patterns of an area over time

C. Cross out the word in each group that does not belong.

1. rain — wind — change — temperature
2. design — style — form — earth
3. mountains — storms — droughts — floods
4. engineer — environment — architect — scientist
5. clothes — shoes — colors — jewelry
6. vary — record — change — alter
7. affect — influence — determine — destroy
8. damage — destroy — learn — ruin
9. extreme — drastic — profound — simple

THE BEAUFORT WIND SCALE

This scale is used to rate how strong the wind is. It was invented in 1805 by a British admiral named Sir Francis Beaufort. The scale rates the speed of wind based on a scale of 0–17.

Beaufort Number	Name for Description of Wind	Miles per Hour	Kilometers per Hour	Effect on Land
0	calm	less than 1	less than 1	smoke rises straight up
1	light air	1–3	1–5	smoke moves slowly with air
2	light breeze	4–7	6–11	wind can be felt on face; leaves rustle
3	gentle breeze	8–12	12–19	leaves and small twigs move; flags wave
4	moderate breeze	13–18	20–28	small branches move; paper blows around
5	fresh breeze	19–24	29–38	small trees move
6	strong breeze	25–31	39–49	large branches move; umbrellas difficult to use
7	moderate gale	32–38	50–61	whole trees move; difficult to walk against the wind
8	fresh gale	39–46	62–74	twigs break off trees; very difficult to walk against the wind
9	strong gale	47–54	75–88	some damage to buildings; shingles blow off roofs
10	whole gale	55–63	89–102	trees pulled out of ground; lots of damage to buildings
11	storm	64–73	103–117	widespread damage
12–17	hurricane	74 and above	more than 117	violent destruction

SELECTION 2

APPLICATION OF INFORMATION

SCANNING

Read the following situations. Then scan the information presented in the Beaufort scale to answer the questions.

1. It's a nice spring day, and you are taking your dog for a walk in your neighborhood. The birds are singing and small branches are blowing in the breeze. You see some papers blowing around on the street and your dog runs after them and tries to catch them.

   What is the Beaufort number for the wind on this day? _____

2. You are walking home from the bus stop. It's raining hard, and you notice that large branches are moving on the trees. You are walking fast trying not to get too wet. Unfortunately, it's difficult to use your umbrella because the wind is blowing.

   How fast do you think the wind is blowing? _____

3. You are sitting on a bench in the park, relaxing after a hard day of work. You can feel the wind on your face and smell the flowers. It's very quiet, and you can hear the leaves rustle.

   What is the name for the description of the wind? _____

4. You are on your way home from school. It isn't very far, but you are having a hard time walking because the wind is blowing so hard. You can tell that a storm is coming. A twig breaks off a tree and almost hits you.

   What is the Beaufort number of the wind? _____

5. It's a beautiful winter day. The snow has just fallen and everything looks white and clean. The air smells fresh. You are outside admiring the snow and watching the smoke rise up from the chimneys. It's getting very cold, and you decide to go inside and make a fire.

   How fast do you think the wind is blowing? _____

The hottest place on Earth is Daloi, Ethiopia. The average temperature there is 34° C (94° F). The coldest place on Earth is Polus Nedostupnosti in Antarctica, where the average temperature is −58° C (−72°F).

SELECTION 3

CLIMATE CONTROL / UNIT 5

Dave Cook, a marketing communications consultant, has always been fascinated by the weather. In fact, it has been a hobby of his ever since he was a child. In **What's the Weather?** Mr. Cook discusses how he became interested in the weather and how meteorologists predict it.

BEFORE YOU READ

PREREADING DISCUSSION

1. Do you usually listen to the weather report before you go out in the morning?

2. How accurate are the weather predictions in your city or home town?

What's the Weather?

How did you first get interested in the weather?

1   As a boy, the first thing I did each morning was look at the weather forecast in the newspaper or check it on the radio.

2   When I became an adult, I kept my interest in the radio and TV reports. They have become more and more interesting as the forecasting technology has become better. It was during the 1970s that I finally found my opportunity to become involved. I heard a Boston TV meteorologist reporting rain. I called to tell him that it might be raining at the station but that it was snowing where I lived. The meteorologist asked me if I would be his "weather watcher" for the northwest suburbs. Of course I accepted. As the northwest suburban weather watcher, I call in every morning at 5:30 with the current temperature, sky condition, and precipitation amounts for my area. It really

SELECTION 3

gets interesting during heavy rains, hurricanes, and snowstorms when I might call in every two hours as the conditions change for better or for worse. At times like that, there is a feeling of truly providing a service to the community.

How is the weather predicted?

Weather satellites like this one have cameras that can photograph the entire earth.

3   In the past few years, weather predicting has become more scientific through the use of high technology. Today, as we watch weather forecasts, we see photographs of the Earth that are sent back by satellite transmissions from outer space. In addition, forecasters now have very advanced computer systems available. These systems produce forecasts that are based on actual historical patterns of data. In other words, these computers "know" what has happened in the past when certain atmospheric conditions exist in particular combinations. In this way, the computer can make a model of what will probably happen next. Although these models are not perfect, there have been many successes. An example was the almost perfect forecast—five days in advance—of the major, history-making blizzard that hit the East Coast of the United States in March of 1993. That storm left about eighteen inches of snow on the ground in New England and had hurricane-force winds of over seventy miles per hour. It was typical of the big New England storms that are called "Nor'easters." These storms are very strong. They bring heavy rain or snow and very high winds that blow from the northeast. That means that they pick up strength from the Atlantic Ocean and can do serious damage.

What happens when the computer predicts something that the meteorologists disagree with?

4   I have asked meteorologists what they would do if the computers were forecasting one thing and their training and experience told them something different. Interestingly, they usually answer that they would go against the computers and with their own best judgment.

CLIMATE CONTROL / **UNIT 5**

BUILDING READING SKILLS
REMEMBERING INFORMATION

How much do you remember? Complete the paragraph with information from the interview. You do not have to use the exact words from the interview. See how many you can do without referring to the text. Then go back and look up the rest of the answers.

Dave Cook has always been interested in _____. It has been his _____ ever since he was a child. Now he is a "weather watcher" for a Boston TV station. He feels he _____ a service to his community. According to Mr. Cook, weather reporting has become more _____ due to improvements in _____. Computers can now _____ what the weather will be, based on historical data. For example, in 1993, computers _____ the huge _____ that hit the East Coast of the United States in March.

EXPANDING VOCABULARY

Circle the letter of the word that is closest in meaning to the underlined word.

1. *It was during the 1970s that I finally found my opportunity to become involved.*

    a. chance
    b. prediction
    c. hobby

2. *At times like that, there is a feeling of truly providing a service to the community.*

    a. checking
    b. interesting
    c. giving

SELECTION 3

An average flash of lightning can provide all the electricity a house needs for two weeks.

3. These systems produce forecasts that are based on <u>actual</u> historical patterns of data.

   a. perfect
   b. real
   c. different

4. An example was the almost perfect forecast—five days in advance—of the major, history-making <u>blizzard</u> that hit the East Coast of the United States in March of 1993.

   a. storm
   b. weather
   c. success

5. That means that they pick up strength from the Atlantic Ocean and can do serious <u>damage</u>.

   a. help
   b. improvement
   c. harm

BUILDING VOCABULARY SKILLS
SUFFIXES

A suffix is a group of letters added to the end of a word to change its meaning. The suffix *-ist* is often added to a word to mean *someone who*. For example a *pianist* is someone who plays the piano, and a *violinist* is someone who plays the violin.

The word *meteorologist* appears in the interview you have just read. Meteorology is the study of weather. What do you think *meteorologist* means?

_____

Study the following examples and do the exercise that follows.

A <u>scientist</u> is someone who studies science.

A <u>tourist</u> is a person who travels for pleasure.

Write a sentence for each word on the list.

1. economist _____

2. specialist _____

CLIMATE CONTROL / UNIT 5

3. dentist _____

4. biologist _____

5. chemist _____

6. psychologist _____

7. chronobiologist _____

BUILDING READING SKILLS
SKIMMING FOR MAIN IDEAS

As you have learned, people read for many different reasons. Sometimes, it is necessary to read quickly, in order to find the general idea of a passage. This is called **skimming**. Keep in mind that when you skim something, you do not need to read every word because you are not interested in the details.

Skim the following newspaper articles about the weather. Try to find the general idea of each article. Then match the article with the appropriate headline. Write the correct headline on the line above the article.

Disaster Brings People Together

IT'S BEEN A LONG, HOT SUMMER

Protect Yourself from the Forces of Nature

KILLER STORM HITS COAST

Bad Weather Brings Good Business

1. _____

Hurricane Babette reached the northeastern United States today and caused death and destruction everywhere. The killer storm carried winds of 135 miles per hour. The high winds and heavy rains combined with the force of the Atlantic Ocean to create extremely dangerous waves. It is not yet known how many people died or were hurt in this storm, but it is estimated that the numbers will be very high. The damage to homes, businesses, and crops will run into the billions of dollars. Now that the storm is over, the long, slow process of rebuilding will begin.

(continued on the next page)

2. _____

With the arrival of the tornado season, the National Weather Service is again telling people how to protect themselves from these deadly storms. The winds from tornadoes are the most violent winds on earth. They can blow up to 400 miles per hour. A tornado looks like a funnel; it is also very loud. It may sound like a train coming at you. In fact, the winds from a tornado can pick up a section of a train and throw it around. If a tornado is seen in your area, it is very important that you protect yourself. A basement is the safest place to go. Try to wait under a table in the basement. If your building does not have a basement, stay on the ground floor but lie flat under a bed or table. Stay away from windows. If you are outside or in your car, try to find a ravine to lie down in.

3. _____

The winter of 1994 was one of the worst in years. By February, there were heavy rains in the South, record-setting snowstorms in the Northeast and Midwest, and problems for most Americans in these areas. Schools, shopping centers, gas stations, and many other services were closed for days at a time. But for some businesses, the cold weather and heavy storms brought big profits. For example, True Value hardware stores sold half a million shovels during the winter of 1994. This was up 75 percent from the year before. Customers also bought 50 million pounds of rock salt, which is used to melt ice. Ice scrapers were another "hot" item. ServiStar's sales of ice scrapers in December, January, and February equaled sales of the past four years combined. Finally, sales of winter clothes were higher than ever. For example, hat sales were up 13 percent, and retailers sold about 95 million pairs of gloves. One company, L.L. Bean, usually sells 150,000 pairs of its most popular winter boot, but during the winter of 1994, it sold over 350,000 pairs.

4. _____

As the area tries to cope with the worst flood of the century, there are many heartwarming stories of people helping other people. From all over the world, people have sent food and clothing to help the thousands who have had to leave their homes. Many volunteers have come to help make sandbags and use them to build walls against the overflowing rivers. While the consequences of this disaster will be terrible for many, it is beautiful to see people coming together to help others and save lives, possessions, and property.

5. _____

As the temperature reaches 96 degrees for the eighth day in a row, thousands of people are escaping the heat by going to the beach. Hotels are full and every available house has been rented. It is not unusual to see portable fax machines, computers, and cellular phones set out like an office on a beach towel. Meteorologists say that they cannot predict when the heat wave will end. Whether you go to the beach or not, they warn of the importance of drinking plenty of liquids. The elderly and those people with respiratory problems should stay inside, with air conditioning if possible. And don't forget that animals suffer also in this kind of heat. Make sure that they have plenty of water.

TYING IT ALL TOGETHER

DISCUSSION

1. Mark Twain, a famous American author, once said, "Everyone talks about the weather, but nobody does anything about it." Why not?

2. A common weather expression is, "If you don't like the weather, wait a minute." Is this true in your country? Why?

3. We have the technology to "seed" clouds to make it rain. Do you think it is a good idea for us to seed clouds where there are droughts?

JUST FOR FUN

WEATHER FOLKLORE

Much folklore about the weather has been passed down from one generation to the next. Some of the following common weather expressions are true, and some are false.

Read each expression and decide whether you think it is true or false. If you think it is true, write *T* on the line provided. If you think it is false, write *F*. Then, check your answers in the Answer Key on page 211.

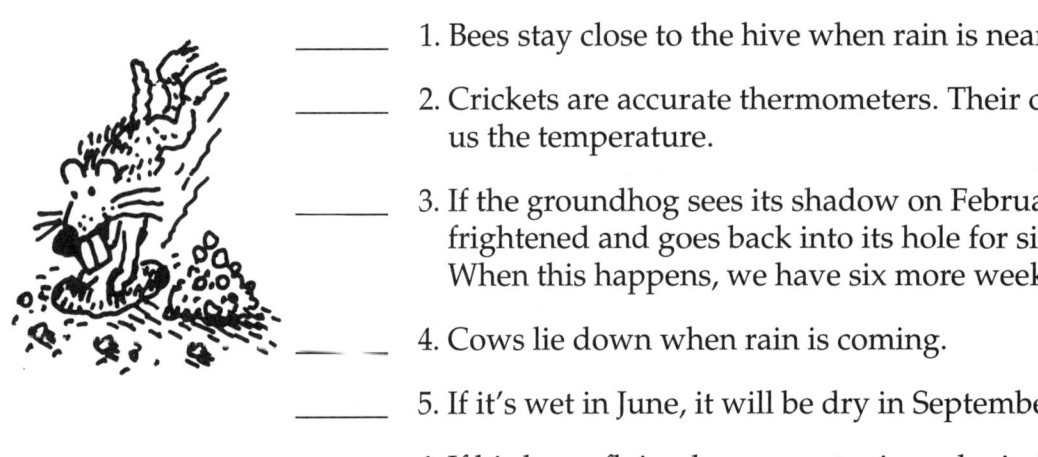

_____ 1. Bees stay close to the hive when rain is near.

_____ 2. Crickets are accurate thermometers. Their chirping can tell us the temperature.

_____ 3. If the groundhog sees its shadow on February 2, it becomes frightened and goes back into its hole for six more weeks. When this happens, we have six more weeks of winter.

_____ 4. Cows lie down when rain is coming.

_____ 5. If it's wet in June, it will be dry in September.

_____ 6. If birds are flying low, expect rain and wind.

_____ 7. If March comes in like a lamb, it will go out like a lion. If it comes in like a lion, it will go out like a lamb.

_____ 8. Pine cones open in dry weather and close in wet weather.

_____ 9. A heavy coat on animals or caterpillars means a long, hard winter is coming.

_____ 10. It's a sign of rain when seagulls sit on beaches.

CLIMATE CONTROL / **UNIT 5**

_____ 11. When squirrels collect many nuts, expect a hard winter.

_____ 12. Red sky at night, sailor's delight. Red sky in the morning, sailors take warning.

What other weather folklore can you add?

13. _____

14. _____

VOCABULARY REVIEW

WORK TOGETHER

In small groups, discuss the meaning of each of the following words from this unit. Write a definition or a synonym for each word. Try not to use your dictionary. Then, as a group, write a sentence for each word that shows you understand the meaning of the word. Share your sentences with the rest of the class.

1. destroy _____

_____

2. vary _____

_____

3. typical _____

_____

4. function _____

_____

5. damage _____

_____

6. meteorologist _____

_____

7. forecast _____

_____

(*continued on the next page*)

TYING IT ALL TOGETHER

8. provide

9. symptom

10. crops

11. severe

12. depressed

13. floods

14. drought

SELF-TEST

In order to answer the following questions, you will need to understand the underlined word. Show that you understand the words by answering the questions in the space provided.

1. What is <u>typical</u> winter weather like in your country?

2. What parts of the world suffer from <u>droughts</u>?

3. What are the most important <u>crops</u> in your country?

4. What are the most common <u>symptoms</u> of SAD?

5. Have you ever seen a place <u>destroyed</u> by a serious storm? When? Where? What kind of storm was it?

6. What kinds of things make you feel <u>depressed</u>?

7. What is the most <u>severe</u> season in your country?

8. Are <u>floods</u> a problem in your country? When? Why?

9. What is the usual <u>function</u> of computers in meteorology?

10. How successful are <u>meteorologists</u> at <u>forecasting</u> the weather in your country?

11. What kind of <u>damage</u> do hurricanes (or earthquakes, floods, blizzards) cause?

12. What are some of the most important things parents should <u>provide</u> for their children?

13. How do your eating habits <u>vary</u> when the seasons change?

READER'S JOURNAL

Think about the topics and ideas you have read about and discussed in this unit. Choose a topic and write about it for ten to twenty minutes. You may pick a topic from the following list or choose one of your own.

- your ideal climate
- the worst storm you have been in
- how the weather affects your mood
- one of the proverbs mentioned in this unit
- your thoughts on one of the questions from the Points to Ponder or Tying It All Together sections.

READER'S JOURNAL

Date: _____

Food For Thought

Unit•6

Selections

1. Finding the Recipe for Success 132
2. Genetically Altered Tomato Approved 136
3. Red Hot, or Not? 140
4. Plant Power 145

English speakers use the expression "food for thought" to describe something that is worth thinking about. As the title of this unit, it refers both to the foods we eat and to some issues concerning food in our daily lives.

POINTS TO PONDER

Answer each of the following questions about yourself. Then discuss your answers in small groups.

1. In your country, do you have special foods that are associated with specific holidays or ceremonies? Make a list of foods that you eat on special occasions, and share it with your classmates.

   _____

   _____

   _____

   _____

2. Think about your eating habits. Put a check mark in the appropriate columns. Then discuss your answers.

	Usually True	Usually False
1. I leave the table feeling very full after meals.	____	____
2. When I order a soda, I get the large size.	____	____
3. When there is a dessert in my house, I eat the whole thing within a few days.	____	____
4. I sometimes eat when I'm not hungry.	____	____
5. I eat a snack before I go to bed.	____	____
6. I don't eat breakfast.	____	____
7. I always get food when I go to the movies.	____	____
8. I drink more coffee during the week than on the weekends.	____	____
9. I eat more when I'm with other people.	____	____
10. I eat when I'm sad, depressed, bored, or nervous.	____	____

FYI

McDonald's serves approximately 13,698,630 hamburgers per day worldwide.

SELECTION 1

Finding the Recipe for Success is an interview with Liz Rozin, a cookbook author and food historian. Liz Rozin writes about eating and cooking behaviors around the world. She is best known for her books *The Flavor-Principle Cookbook, Ethnic Cuisine, Blue Corn and Chocolate,* and *The Primal Cheeseburger.*

BEFORE YOU READ

PREREADING DISCUSSION

1. Do you enjoy eating foods from other cultures? What is your favorite food from another country?

2. Do you like to cook? What is your specialty? Have you ever tried to prepare a dish from another country?

Finding the Recipe for Success

How did you become interested in researching and writing about food?

1   I have always enjoyed eating, but I used to be very unsophisticated about eating and cooking. About twenty-five years ago I had the good fortune to take a trip around the world. That was very important for my early interest in food. When I got home, I wanted to create in my kitchen the foods I had eaten on my trip. Each part of the world has its own distinctive cuisine or style of cooking. As I tried to

recreate these foods, I began to realize that just as people have a system for producing language or art, they also have a system for producing cooked food. If I wanted to produce authentic-tasting food, I needed to understand the mixture of flavorings that characterize a certain cuisine.

2   Every culture has a tendency to use the same flavorings frequently, and they almost always use them in the same way. I learned that the system (the rules and traditions that make each cuisine unique) come from the basic foods available, the cooking methods used, and most importantly, the combination of flavorings used. I call these the "flavor principles." In fact, when I realized that there were systems for preparing ethnic food that could be described and taught, I decided to write my first book, *The Flavor Principle*.

You are the one who developed the "flavor principle" theory of cuisine. How would you describe your theory?

3   Everybody wants their food to taste good or right. But what tastes good or right to one group of people might not taste good or right to another group. When you look at different cuisines throughout the world, what you see is that people in a culture group or country always tend to use specific combinations of ingredients for flavor. For example, in Mexico, the combination of tomatoes with a huge variety of chile peppers is used in almost all cooked food. In Hungary, the combination is onions, lard (pig fat), and paprika. In Asia, soy sauce is widely used. Within the large soy sauce family are many individual traditions: In China, the combination is soy sauce, rice wine, and ginger root. In Korea, it's soy sauce, sesame, and chile. In Indonesia, it's soy sauce, sugar, and peanuts. In Japan, it's soy sauce, sweet rice wine, and sesame or ginger. Each culture has its own unique combination.

How did cuisines develop historically to become so different?

4   Well, that of course is very complicated. In brief, cuisines are historically based on geography, climate, and cultural traditions that were established long ago. These traditions have been passed down from generation to generation. People like to keep what is known and traditional in their cuisines. They all seem to enjoy food that is consistent and familiar. What is really interesting is that people might add new food choices and flavors, but they also keep the old, known traditional foods and flavors.

SELECTION 1

MATCHING

Match each country with the ingredients. Write the correct letter on the line.

COUNTRY	INGREDIENTS
_____ 1. Mexico	a. soy sauce, sesame, chile
_____ 2. Hungary	b. tomatoes, chile peppers
_____ 3. Japan	c. soy sauce, sugar, peanuts
_____ 4. Korea	d. onions, lard, paprika
_____ 5. Indonesia	e. soy sauce, rice wine, ginger

HOW WELL DID YOU READ?

Read each of the following statements. If a statement is true, write *T* on the line. If it is false, write *F*.

_____ 1. Things that taste good to one group of people may not taste good to another group.

_____ 2. Soy sauce is an important ingredient in most Asian cuisines.

_____ 3. Cuisines develop slowly but change very quickly.

_____ 4. Most people enjoy food that is familiar.

_____ 5. Most cultures have a system for producing food.

BUILDING VOCABULARY SKILLS

SUFFIXES AND WORD FORMS

Many verbs can be changed into nouns by adding the suffix *-tion*, for example, *define* and *definition* or *predict* and *prediction*.

Study the following examples and then do the exercise that follows.

Can you define the word cuisine? The definition of cuisine is a style of cooking.

My mother predicted that I would marry a doctor. Her prediction came true.

A. Complete the sentences with the correct form of the word.

1. create   creation

   a. Scientists study about the _____ of the universe.

   b. The band members tried to _____ a new kind of music.

2. realize   realization

   a. Do you _____ how important this assignment is?

   b. He came to the _____ that he should change his major.

3. describe   description

   a. The student had to write a _____ of her favorite movie.

   b. Please try to _____ what happened at the meeting.

4. combine   combination

   a. You need to _____ these ingredients before you add the eggs.
   b. Our class is a _____ of people from many countries.

5. complicate   complication

   a. Janet is late. This will _____ our plans.

   b. It didn't happen the way we planned. There was a _____.

B. Now write sentences of your own using the following words.

1. suggest _____
2. suggestion _____
3. operate _____
4. operation _____
5. immigrate _____
6. immigration _____
7. inform _____
8. information _____
9. select _____
10. selection _____

The average Asian eats more than three hundred pounds of rice per year; the average Westerner eats six pounds.

SELECTION 2

Scientists have been working on ways to improve the foods we eat. In **Genetically Altered Tomato Approved**, you will read about a new kind of tomato that has recently made the news. As you read, think about why they chose the name "Flavr Savr" for this tomato.

BEFORE YOU READ

PREREADING DISCUSSION

1. How do you feel about the fact that scientists are working to improve the color, size, and flavor of some foods?

2. Do you think genetically altered foods can be as safe as natural foods?

Genetically Altered Tomato Approved

1. The Food and Drug Administration (FDA) has approved the first genetically altered food in the U.S. It is a tomato called the Flavr Savr. It will be sold across most of the country within a year.

2. Calgene, Inc., developed the Flavr Savr. The company changed the genes in tomato seeds. The changed seeds produce a tomato that softens more slowly. That means farmers can let it ripen on the vine longer.

3. The new tomato lasts longer and tastes better, says Calgene. It plans to sell the Flavr Savr as a high-priced gourmet tomato.

4. Companies that develop genetically altered food praised the FDA decision. "We think it's terrific news for the industry," said Robert Serenbetz. He heads the DNA Plant Technology Corporation in Oakland, California.

5. The FDA said the Flavr Savr was "as safe as any tomato on the market." It will not require labels telling shoppers the tomato is genetically altered.

FOOD FOR THOUGHT / UNIT 6

6 But some groups say the Flavr Savr should have clear labels. They say no one knows what effects the genetic changes could have.

7 Jeremy Rifkin heads the Pure Food Campaign. "Consumers have a right to know if there is something different in their tomato," he said.

8 FDA rules govern genetically altered foods. The FDA asks companies to inform it about major changes in foods. But it doesn't have any way to check up on the companies.

9 Critics say the FDA should require more facts before a new food is sold. FDA Commissioner David Kessler said his agency is talking about this idea.

10 Other genetically altered foods could be sold soon. They include

- oils with less harmful fat
- grains with more protein
- vegetables that resist disease and need less water
- potatoes that absorb less fat when fried

●●●●●●●●●●●●●●●●●●●●

THINK IT OVER Why do you think this article made the news?

    a. It is reporting the first time the FDA has approved genetically altered food in the United States.

    b. Calgene, Inc., has developed tomato seeds that produce tomatoes that ripen more slowly.

    c. Flavr Savr tomatoes will not have labels that say "genetically altered."

SELECTION 2

HOW WELL DID YOU READ?

Read each of the following statements. If a statement is true, write *T* on the line. If it is false, write *F*.

_____ 1. Flavr Savr tomatoes are genetically altered.

_____ 2. The FDA has approved many genetically altered foods recently.

_____ 3. The new Flavr Savr tomatoes ripen more quickly.

_____ 4. Everyone agrees with the FDA's decision that Flavr Savr tomatoes do not require any special labels.

_____ 5. The FDA does not have any way to check up on companies that make genetic changes in foods.

_____ 6. Flavr Savr tomatoes are cheaper than other tomatoes on the market.

_____ 7. Other genetically altered foods will probably be sold in the future.

_____ 8. According to the FDA, Flavr Savr tomatoes are as safe as any other tomatoes.

BUILDING READING SKILLS

DISTINGUISHING FACT FROM OPINION

Read each of the following statements. If you think a statement is a fact, write *fact* on the line. If you think a statement is someone's opinion, write *opinion* on the line.

_____ 1. Flavr Savr is the first genetically altered food to be approved by the FDA.

_____ 2. Calgene, Inc., has changed the gene in tomato seeds.

_____ 3. The Flavr Savr tomato is as safe as any other tomato on the market.

_____ 4. No one knows what effects the genetic changes could have.

_____ 5. The FDA should require more facts before a new food is sold.

_____ 6. The new Flavr Savr tomato tastes better than other tomatoes.

FOOD FOR THOUGHT / **UNIT 6**

EXPANDING VOCABULARY

Circle the letter of the word that is closest in meaning to the underlined word.

1. *FDA rules govern genetically <u>altered</u> foods.*

   a. priced
   b. changed
   c. informed

2. *It plans to sell the Flavr Savr as a <u>high-priced</u> gourmet tomato.*

   a. expensive
   b. cheap
   c. soft

3. *"We think it's <u>terrific</u> news for the industry," said Robert Serenbetz. He heads the DNA Plant Technology Corporation in Oakland, California.*

   a. unusual
   b. great
   c. terrible

4. *<u>Critics</u> say the FDA should require more facts before a new food is sold.*

   a. opponents
   b. fans
   c. companies

5. *The FDA asks companies to <u>inform</u> it about major changes in foods.*

   a. include
   b. approve
   c. tell

SELECTION 3

Chile peppers are grown in hot, tropical climates all over the world. Centuries ago, chile peppers were used by Aztec and Mayan Indians in South and Central America. They were brought to Africa, India, and the Far East by traders. **Red Hot, or Not?** will give you more interesting information about this fiery fruit.

BEFORE YOU READ

PREREADING DISCUSSION

1. Do you prefer spicy food or mild food?

2. Are chiles part of the cuisine of your country? If they are, what dishes are they used in?

Red Hot, or Not?

1. You're at a restaurant and you bite into a chile pepper. Your eyes start to water. You sniffle. You cough. You sweat. Your heart beats fast. Your lips, tongue, and mouth burn. It feels like your head is going to explode. Your only thought is: Help! How can I put out this fire?

2. Chile peppers are hot. And we don't just mean fiery-tasting. Chile peppers have become *the* food to eat in the U.S. Americans ate more than 165 million pounds of red chile peppers in 1992. And more people in the U.S. now eat salsa—a hot sauce made with chile peppers—than eat ketchup!

3. Chiles may be catching on in the U.S., but they have been popular in other countries for centuries, especially in Mexico, India, and Thailand.

4. So the burning question is: What makes chiles so popular? What is this food that bites back?

The Hot Secret

5. Chile peppers grow on plants. Botanists[1] count the chile pepper as a berry. Horticulturists[2] consider it a fruit because it has seeds. New Mexico, the hot spot of chile peppers in the U.S., has declared it the official state vegetable.

[1] **botanists** Scientists who study plants.
[2] **horticulturists** People who grow plants.

6   No matter what you call it, a chile pepper has to be hot. And what makes it burn is a chemical called capsaicin (*cap-SAY-a-sin*). Capsaicin is an oil found in no other plant. It is colorless and odorless. But if you put one drop of the oil into 100,000 drops of water and drank it, you would still really feel the heat. Here's why it feels like a furnace[1] is in your mouth: In your tongue are sensors that cause you to feel pain from high temperatures. When chiles set off those sensors, the sensors fool you into thinking the pain comes from heat.

7   Some chile peppers are hotter than others. The extra heat has to do with the type—not the amount—of capsaicin oil.

8   Luckily, biting into a pepper isn't the only way to tell how hot a pepper is. A machine can do it. The machine measures the heat of a pepper's capsaicin. The measurements are called Scoville units (named for the man who invented the test). The more Scoville units, the hotter the pepper.

9   A jalapeño pepper measures between 3,500 and 4,500 units. The habanero is the hottest chile pepper in the world. It goes off the scale at 300,000 units.

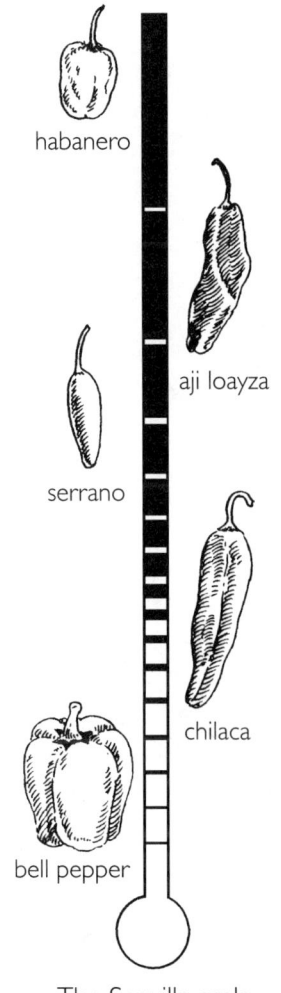

The Scoville scale.

If You Can't Stand the Heat...

10   Okay, so a tabasco pepper measures 50,000 Scoville units. Why eat it?

11   "Eating chile peppers wakes up your tongue," says Melissa Stock, an editor of *Chile Pepper* magazine. "Eating them helps you taste other foods better. The more you eat spicy foods, the more you want to try," she says. "It would be really sad to eat only bland foods like mashed potatoes our whole lives."

12   That's why people put chile peppers in so many foods. They're in salsa—the red sauce you dip tortilla chips in. They're also in tabasco sauce, chili con carne, and spicy chicken wings.

13   Whatever foods they're in, chile peppers make you feel good. The capsaicin releases chemicals in the brain called endorphins. Once endorphins are released, you get a feeling of well-being.

[1] **furnace** An extremely hot place.

SELECTION 3

14 Some people compare eating chiles to riding a roller coaster. You're miserable, even scared, while you do it. But you feel so good afterward! And you can't wait to do it again.

Chile Pepper Prescription?

15 Being hooked on chile peppers may be a good thing. The peppers are packed with vitamins A and D. And some scientists think capsaicin might cure what ails you. For centuries, people all over the world have used chiles to treat head colds (that's why capsaicin is in a special nasal spray for stuffy noses), flu, and asthma.

16 Capsaicin also seems to be a natural pain reliever. Some people rub a watered-down capsaicin oil on their gums to stop toothaches. (The hotness of the capsaicin causes the brain to release pain-relieving messages.) It is used in creams to reduce pain in arthritis and diabetes and to stop itching.

17 Dr. George Daily says, "Capsaicin works as a pain reliever in about 70 percent of the patients I've tried it on." He and other researchers point out that because you put the capsaicin right on the area, instead of taking it by mouth, it doesn't have bad side effects that other medicines sometimes have.

18 Scientists are also studying the use of capsaicin in other illnesses, such as headaches. Research shows that it may also reduce the chance of developing some types of cancer.

19 Not only do chile peppers make people feel better, they make them feel cooler. Eating a chile pepper causes your face and scalp to sweat—and sweating helps you chill out. That's why chile peppers are popular in countries with hot climates.

●●●●●●●●●●●●●●●●●●●●●

HOW WELL DID YOU READ?

Read the following statements. If a statement is true, write *T* on the line. If it is false, write *F*.

_____ 1. Everyone agrees that chile peppers are a fruit.

_____ 2. Eating a chile pepper is the only way to see how hot it is.

_____ 3. Chile peppers are used in many kinds of foods.

_____ 4. Capsaicin is found in many kinds of plants.

_____ 5. People all over the world eat chile peppers to treat colds and flu.

_____ 6. Chile peppers are more popular in cold climates.

FIGURE IT OUT

VOCABULARY IN CONTEXT

Without using your dictionary guess the meaning of the underlined words. Circle the letter of the word or phrase that is closest in meaning to the underlined word in the following sentences.

1. *Chiles may be <u>catching on</u> in the U.S., but they have been popular in other countries for centuries. . . .*

    a. becoming popular
    b. getting better
    c. tasting hotter

2. *"The more you eat spicy foods, the more you want to try. . . . It would be really sad to eat only <u>bland</u> foods like mashed potatoes our whole lives."*

    a. hot
    b. tasteless
    c. expensive

3. *Capsaicin also seems to be a natural pain reliever. . . . It is used in creams to <u>reduce</u> pain in arthritis and diabetes and to stop itching.*

    a. examine
    b. cause
    c. decrease

4. *You're <u>miserable</u>, even scared, while you do it [eat chile peppers]. But you feel so good afterward!*

    a. happy
    b. uncomfortable
    c. excited

5. *And some scientists think that capsaicin might <u>cure</u> what ails you.*

    a. make healthy
    b. disappoint
    c. think about

How do you put out a fire if you eat a chile pepper? Eat bread, rice, yogurt, ice cream, salt, tortillas— but don't drink water. Water just spreads the fiery oil.

SELECTION 3

BUILDING VOCABULARY SKILLS

SYNONYMS AND ANTONYMS

Decide if the following pairs of words are synonyms or antonyms. If they are synonyms, circle S. If they are antonyms, circle A.

1. spicy   bland   S   A
2. happy   miserable   S   A
3. reduce   decrease   S   A
4. artificial   natural   S   A
5. altered   changed   S   A
6. high-priced   expensive   S   A
7. cure   remedy   S   A

BBUILDING VOCABULARY SKILLS

SUFFIXES

The suffix -less is often added to words to mean *without*. In the article about chile peppers, you learned that capsaicin is *colorless* and *odorless*. This means that capsaicin has no color or odor.

The following sentences each contain a word with the suffix -less. Read the sentences and write a definition for the underlined words.

1. Her grandfather is a rich man today. But when he first came to this country, he was penniless.

   _____

2. Our cat is fearless. Even big dogs don't scare her.

   _____

3. My car went out of control on the icy street, and I was powerless to stop it.

   _____

4. The childless couple have been trying to adopt a baby for many years.

   _____

5. After I heard the news, I was so surprised that I was speechless.

   _____

SELECTION 4

FOOD FOR THOUGHT / UNIT 6

Chiles aren't the only plants that can make you feel better. In fact, the use of plants to prevent and cure diseases is nothing new. Almost every ancient culture used plants for medical purposes. Read **Plant Power** and discover why ginger, garlic, and tea are so popular in some cultures.

BEFORE YOU READ

PREREADING QUESTIONS

1. What foods or beverages do you eat or drink when you are sick?
2. Do you eat or drink anything on a regular basis to keep healthy?

Plant Power

Ginger: Ginger is a favorite ingredient in Chinese cooking. It has a strong, spicy, and sweet flavor that is added to many Chinese dishes. People around the world use ginger to make breads, pickles, soft drinks, and desserts as well as to fight disease. Ginger is a good aid for digestion. It also stimulates blood circulation and reduces fever. In addition, ginger has been found to fight colds and cleanse the kidneys. Finally, some people use ginger to soothe painful joints and cure skin infections.

Garlic: The powers of garlic have been praised for thousands of years. The Chinese and Japanese have used garlic for centuries to treat high blood pressure. In fact, the Japanese food and drug administration officially names garlic as a treatment for this condition. The Japanese have also found

evidence that garlic may be helpful in the treatment of stomach ulcers. Cloves of garlic are widely used to fight infections and reduce the risk of heart attacks.

Tea: Tea is one of the most popular drinks all over the world, but it is also a strong medicinal herb. The Chinese have been drinking tea since 3000 B.C. and believe it helps digestion. Green tea, which is popular in Japan, is rich in fluoride and can prevent tooth decay. Green tea has also been shown to fight skin and stomach cancer and help the immune system. People in some cultures put wet green tea leaves on insect bites to reduce itching. Oolong tea is drunk in Korea and other Asian countries to reduce cholesterol levels after a fatty meal. Japanese research suggests that oolong tea may help lower blood pressure and limit the risk of diseases of the blood vessels.

SELECTION 4

BUILDING READING SKILLS
LOCATING INFORMATION

Look back at the descriptions of ginger, garlic, tea, and chiles and write the name of the plant(s) used for each of the following reasons:

1. to lower blood pressure

   _____

2. to fight infections

   _____

3. to aid digestion

   _____

4. to relieve pain

   _____

5. to fight skin and stomach cancer

   _____

6. to soothe painful joints

   _____

7. to cure headaches

   _____

8. to stimulate blood circulation

   _____

9. to fight tooth decay

   _____

10. to help cure stomach ulcers

    _____

11. to reduce itching from insect bites

    _____

12. to reduce risk of heart attacks

___

13. to help the immune system

___

14. to cleanse the kidneys

___

15. to reduce cholesterol levels

___

16. to fight colds

___

TALK IT OVER

DISCUSSION

1. The treatment of diseases with herbs and plants is called *herbalism*. Herbalism is one of the many kinds of traditional medicine that are still popular today. Another example of a traditional form of medicine is the ancient Chinese practice of acupuncture. What other kinds of traditional medicine do you know of? How are they similar to or different from modern medicine?

2. Are there any traditional forms of medicine that are still used in your culture today? What are they? Do you think they are effective?

3. Why do you think some people prefer to use traditional forms of medicine for the prevention and cure of diseases? Why do you think others prefer to rely on modern methods of medicine?

4. Discuss the popular treatments used in your country for the following diseases and ailments:

   a. headaches

   ___

   b. colds

   ___

(continued on the next page)

SELECTION 4

c. insomnia

d. toothaches

e. eye infections

f. fevers

g. acne

h. high blood pressure

i. arthritis

j. stress

TYING IT ALL TOGETHER

FOOD FOR THOUGHT / **UNIT 6**

DISCUSSION

1. Discuss some of the ways that food is important in our lives (other than to stay alive).

2. "Food is our common ground, a universal experience."[1] Discuss this quote with your classmates. How is this statement true for your class?

3. What do you think George Bernard Shaw meant when he said, "There is no love sincerer than the love of food."[2]

4. What can you learn about a culture by studying its food and eating habits?

CLASS PROJECT

COOKBOOK

1. Write down the recipes for two of your favorite dishes.

2. Make a list of the ingredients needed and a step-by-step procedure so that other people will be able to follow the recipe.

3. Make enough copies for everyone in your class.

4. With your classmates, think of a title for your class cookbook and design a cover.

JUST FOR FUN

LAST LETTER FIRST

Below is a list of questions. Each one refers to something we eat. Write the correct answers on the lines. The last letter of the previous answer will always be the first letter of the next answer. Check your answers in the Answer Key on page 211.

Example:

A. What is a synonym for broth? _s_ _o_ _u_ _p_

B. What fruit has a furry skin and is often used to make pies and jellies? _p_ _e_ _a_ _c_ _h_

C. What is a kind of meat that comes from a pig? _h_ _a_ _m_

1. What do we make when we mix lettuce, tomatoes, cucumbers, carrots, and other vegetables together?

___ ___ ___ ___ ___

(continued on the next page)

[1] James Beard, *Beard on Bread*. 1974.
[2] *Man and Superman*, act 1.

TYING IT ALL TOGETHER

2. What is the name for something sweet we eat after a meal?

   ___ ___ ___ ___ ___ ___ ___

3. What is the name for an oriental sauce served on steak or chicken?

   ___ ___ ___ ___ ___ ___ ___ ___

4. What is a frozen dessert that comes in many flavors?

   ___ ___ ___   ___ ___ ___ ___ ___

5. What do vegetarians not eat?   ___ ___ ___ ___

6. What hot beverage do British and Asian people drink a lot of?

   ___ ___ ___

7. What is a thick-skinned, green-colored fruit that is especially popular in Mexico?   ___ ___ ___ ___ ___ ___ ___

8. What fruit is often made into a breakfast drink?

   ___ ___ ___ ___ ___ ___

9. What do we make omelets out of?   ___ ___ ___ ___

10. What is a popular pasta often served with tomato sauce?

    ___ ___ ___ ___ ___ ___ ___ ___ ___

VOCABULARY REVIEW
WORK TOGETHER

In small groups, discuss the meaning of each of the following words from this unit. Write a definition or a synonym for each word. Try not to use your dictionary. Then, as a group, write a sentence for each word that shows you understand the meaning of the word. Share your sentences with the rest of the class.

1. tough _____

_____

2. bland _____ _____

3. reduce _____

4. create _____

5. realize _____

6. high-priced _____

7. alter _____

8. inform _____

9. critics _____

10. terrific _____

11. complicated _____

12. cure _____

(continued on the next page)

TYING IT ALL TOGETHER

13. miserable _____
_____

14. natural _____
_____

15. catch on _____
_____

SELF-TEST The following sentences contain words from this unit. Read them carefully and answer the questions. Then discuss your responses.

1. If you prefer to eat <u>natural</u> foods, would you go to fast-food restaurants very often?

    YES ____   NO ____

2. If you like <u>bland</u> food, would you eat salsa?

    YES ____   NO ____

3. When a plan is very <u>sensible</u>, do you usually give it up?

    YES ____   NO ____

4. If you like to <u>create</u> unusual foods, would you <u>combine</u> ingredients from different cuisines?

    YES ____   NO ____

5. If you don't <u>realize</u> who I am talking about, should I <u>describe</u> her to you?

    YES ____   NO ____

6. Should you buy <u>high-priced</u> clothes and eat at fancy restaurants when you are trying to save money?

    YES ____   NO ____

FOOD FOR THOUGHT / **UNIT 6**

7. If the <u>critics</u> thought the movie was <u>terrific</u>, would they give it bad reviews?

   YES ____   NO ____

8. If you <u>alter</u> your travel plans, should you <u>inform</u> the person who is meeting you at the airport?

   YES ____   NO ____

9. Do you think health experts would <u>promote</u> a low-fat diet and a regular program of exercise?

   YES ____   NO ____

10. If the directions to my house are very <u>complicated</u>, should I draw you a map?

    YES ____   NO ____

11. When you feel <u>miserable</u>, do you like to watch sad movies?

    YES ____   NO ____

12. Should you drink a lot of liquids and get some rest if you are trying to <u>cure</u> a cold?

    YES ____   NO ____

READER'S JOURNAL

Think about the topics and ideas you have read about and discussed in this unit. Choose a topic and write about it for ten to twenty minutes. You may pick a topic from the following list or choose one of your own.

- your impressions of the food from another country
- your opinion about genetically altered food
- a description of your favorite foods
- your thoughts on how the foods you eat affect your health
- your thoughts on one of the questions from the Points to Ponder or Tying It All Together sections

READER'S JOURNAL

Date: _____

Companies With A Conscience

FYI Unit·7

Selections

1. Profits with Principles 157
2. The Scoop on Ben & Jerry's 162
3. Warm and Fuzzy Soda Bottles 167

For some companies, making money is not the only goal. Other goals include social, political, and environmental action. In this unit, you will read about three companies whose creative ideas for action and hard work have been successful.

POINTS TO PONDER

Answer each of the following questions about yourself. Then discuss your answers in small groups.

1. Do you know of any companies that are politically, socially, or environmentally active? Make a list and then describe them to your classmates.

   _____

   _____

   _____

2. Do you think it is appropriate for a business to become involved in social, environmental, or political issues? Why or why not?

SELECTION 1

COMPANIES WITH A CONSCIENCE / **UNIT 7**

An entrepreneur is a person who owns and runs a business. Entrepreneurs develop creative, new ideas and bring them to the marketplace. Anita Roddick is a successful entrepreneur who owns and runs The Body Shop, a company that sells naturally based products for skin and hair. This unusual company is the subject of the following article: **Profits with Principles.**

BEFORE YOU READ

PREREADING DISCUSSION

1. Do you know any successful entrepreneurs? Describe them to your classmates.

2. What qualities do you think make someone a successful entrepreneur? Make a list of those qualities. Share your list with your classmates.

Profits with Principles

1   Anita Roddick, founder of The Body Shop, was trained as a school teacher. She didn't know anything about the cosmetics industry when she opened her first small shop in Brighton, England, in 1976. But she had good ideas, and people liked her products. Her business grew quickly. Because of her energy, determination, and vision, Anita Roddick has become an international success story. She is one of the five richest women in England. Today, there are over 1,300 branches of The Body Shop in forty-five countries around the world.

2   The Body Shop manufactures and sells over 400 different naturally based products. Anita learns how people from traditional cultures use plants and herbs from their environment to take care of their bodies. In Sri Lanka, for example, she learned that women rub fresh pineapple on their skin to make it softer and smoother. With that knowledge, she created a face product using pineapple. In Polynesia, she learned about many of the uses of cocoa butter. It makes the skin softer and the hair shinier. Cocoa Butter Hand and Body Lotion is one of The Body Shop's best-selling products.

3   The philosophy of The Body Shop is different from the philosophy of most cosmetics companies. It does not promise miracles or ever-

lasting youth. The Body Shop develops its line of high-quality, sensible products by using traditional wisdom, herbal knowledge, and modern technology.

4   The Body Shop does not believe in profits without principles. A respect for the environment is one of The Body Shop's most basic principles. The company uses as little packaging as possible to conserve natural resources and reduce waste. Customers are encouraged to bring their old containers to the shop to refill them. If they do this, they get a discount on their next purchase. The Body Shop is also strongly opposed to animal testing in the cosmetics industry. It never tests its products or ingredients on animals.

5   Helping communities in need is another principle. All employees are encouraged to do volunteer work with local groups. The Body Shop gives employees four hours off each month to do their community work. Some projects include working with homeless people and AIDS victims. The Body Shop also provides educational programs for its staff and customers.

6   The Body Shop has set up trade partnerships with communities in need around the world. "Trade Not Aid" is a cornerstone[1] of the company. For example, The Body Shop has made an agreement with the Kayapo Indians, who harvest Brazil nuts in the Amazon rain forest. The Body Shop uses these nuts in one of its products, Brazil Nut Oil Conditioner for hair. The agreement has several goals. One is to protect the plants the Kayapo Indians harvest from the rain forest. Another goal is to make sure that the Kayapo get the economic benefits from any commercial development in their area. There are similar agreements with communities in India, Mexico, Nepal, Tanzania, and Zambia.

7   Although some of Anita Roddick's ideas for The Body Shop seem unusual for the business world, she must be doing something right. In 1994/5, The Body Shop's International profits were over $34 million.

[1] **cornerstone** Something of great importance.

COMPANIES WITH A CONSCIENCE / UNIT 7

HOW WELL DID YOU READ?

Read the following statements. If a statement is true, write *T* on the line. If it is false, write *F*.

_____ 1. Anita Roddick studied business in school.

_____ 2. The Body Shop is a very successful business.

_____ 3. Many of the ideas for The Body Shop's products come from traditional cultures around the world.

_____ 4. The philosophy of The Body Shop is similar to the philosophies of most other cosmetics companies.

_____ 5. One of The Body Shop's most important principles is respecting the environment.

BUILDING READING SKILLS

SCANNING FOR DETAILS

Read the following questions about The Body Shop. Then scan the article to find the answers. Work as quickly as possible. Do not read every word in the article. As soon as you find the answer to a question, move on to the next one.

1. When did the first Body Shop open? _____

2. How many branches of The Body Shop are there in the world today?
   _____

3. How many countries have branches of The Body Shop?
   _____

4. Approximately how many kinds of products does The Body Shop make and sell? _____

5. Where did Anita learn about the uses of cocoa butter?
   _____

6. Where do the Kayapo Indians live? _____

7. What were The Body Shop's recent International profits in 1994/5?
   _____

SELECTION 1

TALK IT OVER

DISCUSSION

1. Why do you think The Body Shop has become so successful?
2. How does Anita Roddick get ideas for The Body Shop's products? Do you think this is a good way? Why or why not?
3. How is the philosophy of The Body Shop different from that of most other cosmetics companies? Do you agree with The Body Shop's philosophy? Why or why not?
4. In what ways does The Body Shop show its respect and concern for the environment?
5. What types of things does The Body Shop do to help communities in need?
6. What do you think "Trade Not Aid" means?

EXPANDING VOCABULARY

Circle the letter of the word that best completes each sentence.

1. The Body Shop is part of the _____ industry.
   a. traditional
   b. cosmetics
   c. environment

2. The company tries to _____ natural resources by using as little packaging as possible.
   a. conserve
   b. spend
   c. oppose

3. Many of the _____ for The Body Shop's products come from different countries around the world.
   a. goals
   b. cultures
   c. ingredients

4. The Body Shop _____ over 400 kinds of skin and hair products.
   a. manufactures
   b. buys
   c. protects

5. The Body Shop _____ the use of animals for testing in the cosmetics industry.

   a. trains
   b. opposes
   c. believes in

6. Customers who use The Body Shop's products do not expect _____.

   a. miracles
   b. wisdom
   c. profits

7. Many of The Body Shop's employees do _____ work in their communities.

   a. commercial
   b. traditional
   c. volunteer

8. When customers bring in their old _____ to the shop for refills, they get a discount.

   a. products
   b. containers
   c. cosmetics

9. One goal of The Body Shop's trade partnerships is to _____ the Amazon rain forest.

   a. oppose
   b. manufacture
   c. protect

SELECTION 2

Mitch Curren is the Coordinator of Public Relations for Ben & Jerry's, a successful ice cream company in Burlington, Vermont. In the following interview, **The Scoop on Ben & Jerry's,** Ms. Curren talks about some of the ways that Ben & Jerry's is unique.

BEFORE YOU READ

PREREADING ACTIVITY

Look at this excerpt from the cover of *Ben & Jerry's: The Inside Scoop*, by Fred Lager. Then answer the questions that follow with your classmates.

In 1978, with a total investment of $12,000, Ben Cohen and Jerry Greenfield opened a homemade ice cream parlor in an abandoned gas station in Burlington, Vermont, and set out to serve the best ice cream they could make. Less than 15 years later, Ben & Jerry's has grown into a national phenomenon, with annual sales of over $100 million.

But Ben & Jerry's wasn't just another success story, it was a whole new kind of company. First, the founders believed that work should be rewarding in itself. Their unofficial motto was, "If it's not fun, why do it?" Second, they believed that business should give something back to the community that supports it. They started by giving away free ice cream and sponsoring local festivals, but as the company grew, their efforts became more ambitious, and Ben & Jerry's was soon recognized as one of the most progressive, socially active companies in America.

---

1. What do you think Ben and Jerry meant by their motto, "If it's not fun, why do it?" Do you think this was a good motto for a new business? Why or why not?

2. Do you agree with the idea that business should give something back to the community that supports it?

COMPANIES WITH A CONSCIENCE / UNIT 7

The Scoop on Ben & Jerry's

How did Ben & Jerry's get started?

1. Ben Cohen and Jerry Greenfield have been friends since they were in seventh grade. That was in 1963. In 1977, they decided to start an ice cream business together. They took a $5 course to learn how to make ice cream. Then, they opened their first ice cream parlor in Burlington, Vermont, in 1978. Jerry's job was to make the ice cream and to make sure it tasted better than anybody else's ice cream. Ben's job was to sell the ice cream and make sure that everyone knew that Ben & Jerry's ice cream was the best ice cream in the world.

2. They both ate a lot of their ice cream because that was the best way to figure out how good it was. They tried different things and experimented with unusual flavors and recipes for their ice cream. They decided to make ice cream flavors with lots of big chunks of cookies, candies, fruits, and nuts. Ben and Jerry's ideas, and their rich, creamy, chunky ice cream made their business very popular, very fast.

What made Ben & Jerry's such a big success?

3. Ben and Jerry figured out the secret to making great ice cream. They started with fresh milk and cream and added lots of natural flavorings, lots of big chunks, and lots of imagination. To get people to try their product, Ben and Jerry gave out free samples of ice cream everywhere they went. Their plan worked. The more ice cream they gave away, the more new customers they got.

4   Ben and Jerry wanted to run their business with goals that were different from the goals of traditional businesses. Traditional businesses usually have one main goal—to make a lot of money. Ben & Jerry's has three main goals: to make great products, to make money, and to share that money with the community. Ben and Jerry believe that as business prospers, the community prospers too. They call this idea "linked prosperity."

What makes Ben & Jerry's such an unusual business?

5   Our belief that all businesses have a responsibility to give something back to their communities was a very unusual idea several years ago when we first started talking about it. Some people thought we were crazy. They told us that no business could ever succeed and make big profits if it kept giving away the profits to the community. We decided to try it and soon we were able to prove that we weren't as crazy as people thought.

6   Here are some examples of things we've done and are still doing. First of all, every year we give away 7.5 percent of our pretax profits to groups working for the needs of their community. So far, we've given away more than $3 million. But we feel like we've just begun! We also give away lots of ice cream every year. We donate it to charitable groups, food shelves,[1] and community events. In addition, we buy our ingredients from suppliers whose business goals are a lot like ours. For example, we get our brownies from a bakery that employs formerly homeless men and people recovering from drug and alcohol addiction. We get our coffee flavorings from a special cooperative[2] run by Mexican farmers. We buy our cookie dough chunks from another socially responsible company in Vermont.

What else do you do that makes Ben & Jerry's a special kind of company?

7   Well, Ben & Jerry's employees love a good party. So, every year we have huge parties called "One World, One Heart Festivals." This is our way of thanking all our customers while celebrating with them. Tens of thousands of people come to our free festivals to listen to famous musical groups, to eat our ice cream, and to join us in "Social Action Campaigns." These Social Action Campaigns encourage the U.S. government to spend more money on programs that help people who are in need.

The average North American eats about 32 quarts (35.2 liters) of ice cream per year.

[1] **food shelves** Places where food is free for people who need it.
[2] **cooperative** An organization owned by the people who use it and work in it.

COMPANIES WITH A CONSCIENCE / **UNIT 7**

BUILDING READING SKILLS

IDENTIFYING MAIN IDEAS

Which of the following topics are discussed in the interview? Put a check mark next to those topics.

_____ 1. how Ben and Jerry got people to try their product

_____ 2. the company's main goals

_____ 3. Ben & Jerry's competition

_____ 4. examples of the company's social action

_____ 5. the company's history

_____ 6. the nutritional value of Ben & Jerry's ice cream

HOW WELL DID YOU READ?

Match each topic with its explanation. Write the correct letter on the line.

TOPIC

_____ 1. Ben's job

_____ 2. Ben & Jerry's main goals

_____ 3. Ben & Jerry's secret

_____ 4. Jerry's job

_____ 5. linked prosperity

_____ 6. what made Ben & Jerry's very popular, very fast

EXPLANATION

a. start with fresh milk and cream, lots of natural flavorings, lots of big chunks, lots of imagination

b. to make ice cream and make sure it tasted great

c. sharing money with the community so as the business prospers, the community prospers too

d. to make great products, to make money, and to find ways to share that money with the community

e. Ben and Jerry's great ideas and rich, creamy, chunky ice cream

f. to sell the ice cream and make sure everyone knew it was great

SELECTION 2

BUILDING VOCABULARY SKILLS

VOCABULARY IN CONTEXT

With a partner, try to guess the meaning of the underlined words. Use the information in the sentences to figure out the meaning. Do not use your dictionary. Circle the letter of the word or phrase that is closest in meaning to the underlined word in each sentence.

1. *They tried different things and <u>experimented with</u> unusual flavors and recipes for their ice cream.*

   a. bought
   b. tried
   c. threw away

2. *They decided to make ice cream flavors with lots of big <u>chunks</u> of cookies, candies, fruits, and nuts.*

   a. pieces
   b. copies
   c. bowls

3. *To get people to try their product, Ben and Jerry gave out free <u>samples</u> of ice cream everywhere they went. . . . The more ice cream they gave away, the more new customers they got.*

   a. small amounts to taste
   b. something to buy
   c. an unusual idea

4. *Ben & Jerry's has three main goals: to make great products, to make money, and to share that money with the community. Ben and Jerry believe that as business <u>prospers</u>, the community <u>prospers</u> too.*

   a. responds
   b. grows weak
   c. becomes successful

5. *We also give away lots of ice cream every year. We <u>donate</u> it to charitable groups, food shelves, and community events.*

   a. buy
   b. give
   c. sell

The best-selling flavor of Ben & Jerry's ice cream is chocolate chip cookie dough, with approximately 9.6 million pints (5,285,760 liters) sold annually.

SELECTION 3

COMPANIES WITH A CONSCIENCE / **UNIT 7**

Patagonia is an outdoor clothing company that was started in the 1960s by Yvon Chouinard, an entrepreneur with a vision. In **Warm and Fuzzy Soda Bottles,** you will read about how Patagonia is committed to helping the environment.

BEFORE YOU READ

PREREADING QUESTIONS

1. Do you enjoy outdoor activities such as rock climbing, running, sailing, hiking, or biking? If so, which ones?
2. Based on the title, "Warm and Fuzzy Soda Bottles," what do you think the article might be about? Take a guess. You may be surprised.

Warm and Fuzzy Soda Bottles

1. Yvon Chouinard loves the outdoors. He surfs, climbs rocks, skis, hikes, kayaks, and runs Patagonia, a multimillion dollar company. Although Mr. Chouinard does all of these things very well, his real passion is saving the earth. In fact, Mr. Chouinard says he had two reasons for starting his company. First, he wanted to earn enough money so he could become an active environmental philanthropist.[1] And second, he wanted the freedom to spend as much time as possible enjoying nature.

2. Patagonia designs and distributes clothing for use in extreme outdoor weather conditions. It originally started in the 1960s as a climbing and mountaineering equipment company. Yvon Chouinard used to manufacture climbing hardware and sell it out of the back of his car up in the mountains. He then moved on to selling clothing for use in the mountains. All of his products continue to be designed for comfort, simplicity, and versatility.

3. Mr. Chouinard's business grew rapidly, and in 1994, its sales reached $125 million. Patagonia's clothing is popular because it is versatile, comfortable, dries quickly, and remains warm even when it is wet. It works well in hot, cold, wet, dry, humid, arid, windy, and calm weather. Patagonia products are sold around the world through its mail-order catalog.

[1]philanthropist Someone who gives a lot of money to charity.

SELECTION 3

4   In addition to its commitment to providing high-quality products to its customers, Patagonia is also committed to the environment. It pledges one percent of its sales each year to the preservation and restoration of the natural environment. With recent annual sales of $125 million, the company gave $1.2 million to environmental groups around the world.

5   In the early 1990s, Patagonia acknowledged in its catalog that every product Patagonia designed and distributed polluted the earth in some way. The company decided to decrease the impact of its products on the environment and to help people learn more about environmental problems. As a result, in the fall of 1993, Patagonia introduced a new product, a sweater made of recycled soda bottles! The warm, soft, fuzzy fabric was called PCR (*P*ost-*C*onsumer *R*ecycled) Synchilla™. (*Post-consumer recycled* refers to products that have been used by people before.) Because soda bottles are made from very high-quality plastic, it is possible to melt the bottles and make them into yarn for clothes.

6   It takes twenty-five two-liter bottles to make each sweater. The result is that for each sweater made, twenty-five fewer soda bottles go into a landfill[2] somewhere. In addition, it takes less energy and fewer natural resources to make PCR Synchilla™ than it does to make virgin (new) polyester. The first sweaters were made of 80 percent PCR-Synchilla™ and 20 percent virgin polyester. Within a year, the technology had improved and the ratio became 90 percent PCR-Synchilla™ and 10 percent virgin polyester in some products. This meant that more soda bottles were needed to produce an item, so fewer bottles went into landfills. Patagonia's PCR-Synchilla™ products help people see and understand the positive results of recycling. In fact, Patagonia was so determined to share this new technology that it did not patent[3] the process. It hopes that other companies will also use it.

---

[2] **landfill**   A place where trash is buried.
[3] **patent**   To protect from being copied or sold by those who do not have a right to do so.

7   In addition to innovations in the technology of making fabrics, Patagonia has also been urging people to simplify their lives and recycle clothes they don't need. The company tries to make its products as multifunctional as possible. For example, rather than having one pair of shorts to play volleyball in and four other pairs for basketball, kayaking, hiking, and running, Patagonia offers one pair which can be used in a variety of sports under a variety of conditions. This means more space in your closet and less trash in landfills.

8   Patagonia is committed to sharing the issue of environmental responsibility with other businesses. Mr. Chouinard, the board of directors, and the employees think of the company as a tool for social change. It is their hope that more companies will recognize the environmental "costs" of doing business and try to be more planet-friendly.

● ● ● ● ● ● ● ● ● ● ● ● ● ● ● ● ● ● ● ●

BUILDING SKILLS
IDENTIFYING MAIN IDEAS

In small groups, make a list of the main ideas of the article. Then write your lists on the chalkboard and compare them.

_____

_____

_____

BUILDING READING SKILLS
SCANNING FOR DETAILS

Read the following questions about Patagonia. Then scan the article to find the answers. Try to work quickly. Do not reread every word in the article. As soon as you find the answer to a question, move on to the next one.

1. Who owns Patagonia? _____

2. What did the company sell in the 1960s? _____

3. When did Patagonia's sales reach $125 million? _____

4. Why is Patagonia's clothing popular? _____

5. What percent of its sales does Patagonia give to environmental causes?

_____

(continued on the next page)

SELECTION 3

6. How many two-liter bottles does it take to make one PCR-Synchilla™ sweater? _____

7. What percent of virgin polyester was used in the first PCR-Synchilla™ sweaters? _____

HOW WELL DID YOU READ? Patagonia is committed to designing practical clothing that does not have a negative impact on the environment. The following statements describe the reasons behind and the results of some of Patagonia's work.

1. Read this list of reasons:

    - Patagonia wanted to decrease the impact of its products on the environment.
    - Patagonia wants people to simplify their lives.
    - It takes twenty-five two-liter bottles to make each PCR-Synchilla™ sweater.
    - Patagonia's clothes are versatile and comfortable.
    - Patagonia does not intend to patent the process for making fabric from soda bottles.
    - Patagonia improved the technology for making PCR-Synchilla™.
    - Patagonia is committed to the environment.

2. Read the list of results that have been written in the result spaces below.

3. Decide which reason from above led to each result below. Write the correct reason in the appropriate reason arrow.

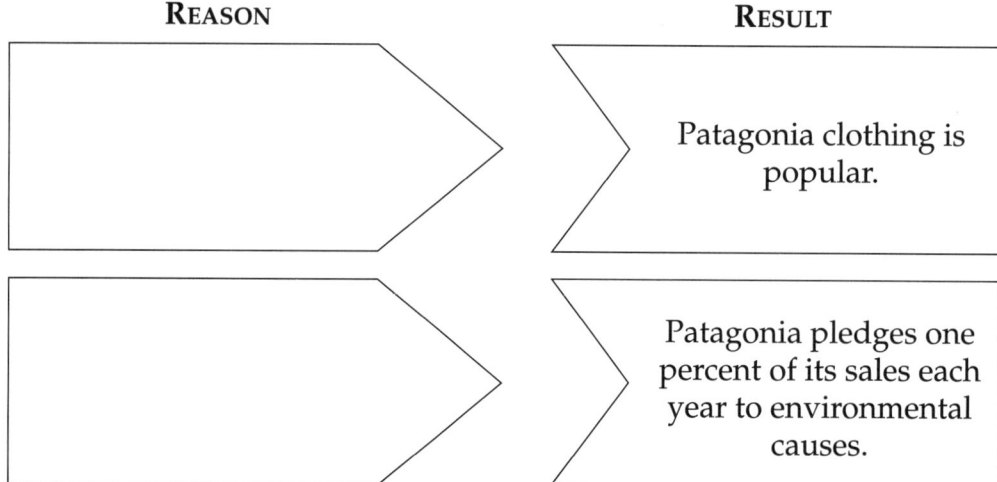

REASON → RESULT: Patagonia clothing is popular.

REASON → RESULT: Patagonia pledges one percent of its sales each year to environmental causes.

COMPANIES WITH A CONSCIENCE / **UNIT 7**

REASON | **RESULT**

→ Patagonia developed PCR-Synchilla™ to use in making sweaters.

→ Fewer bottles go into landfills.

→ Other companies will be able to use it.

→ Patagonia products are as multifunctional as possible.

→ The new ratio for PCR-Synchilla™ is 9 to 1.

FYI

It is estimated that 45 percent of North Americans recycle bottles and cans, but they consume the equivalent of five times their own weight in paper annually.

171

SELECTION 3

READ AND REACT

Read the following statements made by Yvon Chouinard. Then in small groups, discuss your reactions to them.

1. "The measly million or so that we're giving away each year isn't very much money. But I think we're having a tremendous influence on other corporations."[1]

2. "I don't think corporate America realizes how serious people are about the environment. They're scared to death."[2]

3. "Civilization is out of control, growing way beyond its resources, and it will destroy itself."[3]

BUILDING VOCABULARY SKILLS

SYNONYMS OR ANTONYMS

Decide if the following pairs of words are synonyms or antonyms. If they are synonyms, circle *S*. If they are antonyms, circle *A*.

1. versatile	multifunctional		S	A
2. humid	arid		S	A
3. pledge	promise		S	A
4. impact	effect		S	A
5. extensive	limited		S	A
6. recognize	realize		S	A
7. ratio	proportion		S	A
8. committed	dedicated		S	A

BUILDING VOCABULARY SKILLS

PREFIXES

Another prefix that is commonly used in English is *re-*. When *re-* is put in front of a verb, it usually means *to do something again*. For example, the word *rebuild* means to build again:

We had to <u>rebuild</u> our house after the earthquake.

In this unit, you have seen the prefix *re-* several times:

1. *Customers are encouraged to bring their old containers to the shop to <u>refill</u> them.*

2. *Patagonia has also been urging people to simplify their lives and <u>recycle</u> clothes they don't need.*

---
[1] *The Chronicle of Philanthropy*, June 1, 1993, p. 10.
[2] *The Chronicle of Philanthropy*, June 1, 1993, p. 12.
[3] *Los Angeles Times*, Jan. 28, 1994.

COMPANIES WITH A CONSCIENCE / **UNIT 7**

You have done many vocabulary exercises in this book. Now it is your turn to create some. In small groups, talk about the definition of each of the following words. Then write a vocabulary exercise using the words in the list. When you have finished, give your exercise to another group to complete.

> reprint   redecorate   rearrange   refuel   reread

BUILDING VOCABULARY SKILLS

WORD FORMS

Complete each sentence with the correct word.

1. ambitious   ambition

   a. You need a lot of _____ to start your own business.

   b. Anita Roddick is a very _____ person.

2. imagine   imagination

   a. It took a lot of hard work and _____ to complete this project.

   b. Can you _____ a world without poverty and war?

3. progress   progressive

   a. He is working hard and making a lot of _____ on his research.

   b. This is a very _____ school. It uses the most modern teaching methods.

4. responsible   responsibility

   a. It is your _____ to remember to do all your assignments on time.

   b. I really trust my babysitter; she is very _____.

5. celebration   celebrate

   a. We had a big _____ when our son graduated from high school.

   b. I won the lottery. Let's _____!

(continued on the next page)

SELECTION 3

6. encourage   encouragement

   a. Children need a lot of _____, especially when they are trying something new.

   b. Teachers should _____ their students to be creative thinkers.

7. conserve   conservation

   a. It is important to _____ resources like water and electricity.

   b. Many governments believe in the _____ of their country's wildlife.

8. oppose   opposition

   a. We _____ the city's plan to cut down so many trees.

   b. There is a lot of _____ to the university's plan to raise tuition.

9. protect   protection

   a. These boots are good _____ against rain and snow.

   b. Mothers and fathers try to _____ their young children.

10. preserve   preservation

    a. We are committed to the _____ of our environment.

    b. It is important to _____ our valuable natural resources.

11. distributes   distribution

    a. The company _____ its products in many countries.

    b. Who is responsible for the _____ of the prizes?

COMPANIES WITH A CONSCIENCE / **UNIT 7**

12. versatile   versatility

   a. Plastic is a _____ material.

   b. She is known for her _____ as a performer.

13. comfort   comfortable

   a. My shoes are very _____.

   b. I buy my shoes for _____ rather than style.

14. environment   environmental

   a. We need to learn more about _____ problems.

   b. Everyone should be concerned about the _____.

HOW WELL DID YOU READ? The three companies you read about sell different products, but they share some of the same goals. Read the following list and write the name of the company that each item applies to. Some statements may be true for more than one company, and others may not be true for any of them. If the statement does not apply to any of the three companies, leave it blank.

The Body Shop • Ben & Jerry's • Patagonia

_____ 1. makes and sells ice cream

_____ 2. opened its first shop in England

_____ 3. sells its products in many countries

_____ 4. manufactures and sells cosmetics

_____ 5. gives away lots of free samples

_____ 6. uses soda bottles to make sweaters

_____ 7. uses natural ingredients

_____ 8. operates like a traditional business

_____ 9. is committed to helping the environment

(continued on the next page)

SELECTION 3

_____ 10. designs and distributes clothing

_____ 11. opened its first shop in Vermont

_____ 12. sponsors festivals to thank customers

_____ 13. believes that business should give something back to the community that supports it

_____ 14. promises miracles for those who use its products

APPLICATION OF INFORMATION Read the information on the following business cards.

Culture and Cuisine
catering to all your cooking needs
Judy Norris-Porter
phone/fax: 617-792-1678

Tutoring in Reading, Math, Science
Dave Potsaid
25 Windy Way
Gainesville, Florida 32611
phone: 904-627-8369

Apple Tree Publishing Company
Jill Jameson, Editor, New Fiction

36 Monroe Place
New York, NY
10012

212-876-6985
Voice Mailbox: # 629

Pat Ridley
Instructor, English as a Second Language

301 North Main Street
Dayton, Ohio 45426

Phone/fax:
513-371-1000
Extension 2311

COMPANIES WITH A CONSCIENCE / **UNIT 7**

Charles Brooks
PSYCHOLOGIST

2 Pennsylvania Avenue
Stanford, California 94305
Phone: 415-865-2478
Office Hours by Appointment

Weinstein and Davis Real Estate

Fran Davis

209 Stetson Avenue
Portland, Oregon 97034   503-351-9151

LANGUAGE TRAINING ASSOCIATES
TRAINING LANGUAGE TEACHERS AND LEARNERS
FOR OUR SHRINKING WORLD

Brigitte de L'école
FRENCH LANGUAGE TRAINER

141 Industry Avenue
San Antonio, Texas 78203   210-365-5891

Shortman Publishing Group

Walter Ward, Sales Representative
Textbook Order Department

638 Vail Street
Denver, Colorado 80235
1-800-215-4716

Read the situations that follow. Then scan the information in the business cards to answer the question at the end of each situation.

1. You are the director of the English as a second language program at your school. You want to order 100 copies of a writing book and 100 copies of a pronunciation book. What number should you call?

   _____

2. Your son was sick and missed a week of school. He is doing well in most of his classes. In math, however, he is having a lot of trouble because of the work he missed when he was sick. Who can you call for help?

   _____

(continued on the next page)

SELECTION 3

3. You have just been promoted to vice president of your company. In your new job, you will have to travel a lot—mostly to Paris, France. In fact, you will leave next month for Paris and stay there for about two months. You want to learn some French before you go. Who should you call?

   _____

4. You moved to the area a few months ago. You thought that it would be easy to learn English from friends. Now you realize that you need to take an ESL class if you are really going to learn to speak, understand, read, and write English well. Where should you go?

   _____

5. You have decided to have a class party. Since all of you live in dormitories, it will be very difficult for you to cook for the party. A friend told you about a wonderful caterer who specializes in interesting international foods at reasonable prices. What is the phone number of the caterer?

   _____

6. You have recently moved to this area and want to rent an apartment. You need to have someone show you some of the apartments that are available in your price range. Who should you call?

   _____

7. Your daughter is having a lot of trouble learning to read. Her teacher says that she is very intelligent but seems to have trouble sounding out words. She has suggested that you take her to be tested for a reading disability. Who should you take her to see?

   _____

8. You have a great idea for a mystery novel. In fact, you have written the first three chapters of the book, and you would like to have an expert evaluate it. Who would you call?

   _____

TYING IT ALL TOGETHER

COMPANIES WITH A CONSCIENCE / **UNIT 7**

DISCUSSION

1. Anita Roddick has said, "Business people have got to be the instigators of change. They have the money and power to make a difference. A company that makes a profit from society has a responsibility to return something to that society." Do you agree with her? Why or why not?

2. Have you ever had an idea that you thought would make a good business? If so, what was it? Explain the idea to your classmates.

3. Small group activity: Think of an idea for a new business. Discuss it with your group members and make a list of goals for the business.

_____

_____

_____

JUST FOR FUN
WORD PLAY

Look at the word RESPONSIBILITY. It has fourteen letters. Using only these fourteen letters, make as many other words as you can. You may not use the same letter twice unless it appears twice in the word. Do not use proper names or foreign words. Write the words here as you think of them.

Example: _tie_

TYING IT ALL TOGETHER

VOCABULARY REVIEW
WORK TOGETHER

In small groups, discuss the meaning of each of the following words from this unit. Write a definition or a synonym for each word. Try not to use your dictionary. Then, as a group, write a sentence for each word that shows you understand the meaning of the word. Share your sentences with the rest of the class.

1. protect _____

2. ratio _____

3. pledge _____

4. prosper _____

5. motto _____

6. ambitious _____

7. volunteer _____

8. progressive _____

9. miracle _____

10. extensive _____

11. prosperous _____

12. donate _____

13. commitment _____

14. versatile _____

15. conserve _____

16. abandon _____

SELF-TEST

In order to answer the following questions, you will need to understand the underlined words. Show that you understand the words by answering the questions in the space provided.

1. What would you do if you found an <u>abandoned</u> kitten at your door?
   _____

2. Name three ways that we can <u>protect</u> the environment.
   _____

3. What is the <u>ratio</u> of men to women in your class?
   _____

(continued on the next page)

TYING IT ALL TOGETHER

4. Do you believe in <u>miracles</u>? Why or why not?

5. What do you think is the most <u>prosperous</u> company in your country?

6. What is the most <u>versatile</u> piece of clothing that you own? Why?

7. Write a <u>motto</u> for your class or school.

8. The three companies that you read about in this unit are all <u>progressive</u>. What is the most progressive company in your country? In what ways is it progressive?

9. What are some important <u>commitments</u> that you have made in your life?

10. Who is the most <u>ambitious</u> person you know? What makes him or her so ambitious?

11. What are some things in the environment that are important to <u>conserve</u>?

12. Have you ever done any <u>volunteer</u> work? If yes, what kind? If no, what kind would you like to do?

READER'S JOURNAL

Think about the topics and ideas you have read about and discussed in this unit. Choose a topic and write about it for ten to twenty minutes. You may pick a topic from the following list or choose one of your own.

- an unusual business idea that you know about
- socially conscious businesses in your country
- the qualities of a successful entrepreneur
- your thoughts on one of the questions from the Points to Ponder or Tying It All Together sections

TYING IT ALL TOGETHER

READER'S JOURNAL

Date: _____

TUNE IN TO TV

Unit·8

Selections

1. The Early Days and Beyond 187
2. Can You Imagine a World without It? 192
3. Commercial-Free TV 196

Television is often called the machine that brings the world into your home. Whether you are in the mood to learn, laugh, cry, think, or relax, you can usually find something to watch on TV. It offers something of interest to almost everyone.

POINTS TO PONDER

Answer each of the following questions about yourself. Then discuss your answers in small groups.

1. What kinds of television shows do you enjoy most?
2. On the average, how much TV do you watch each day? Each week?
3. Do you find watching TV relaxing? Do you keep the television on in the background even if you aren't really watching it?
4. Do you like to watch commercials? Do you think they are informative or do you find them annoying?
5. What are the differences between TV in your country and in the United States?

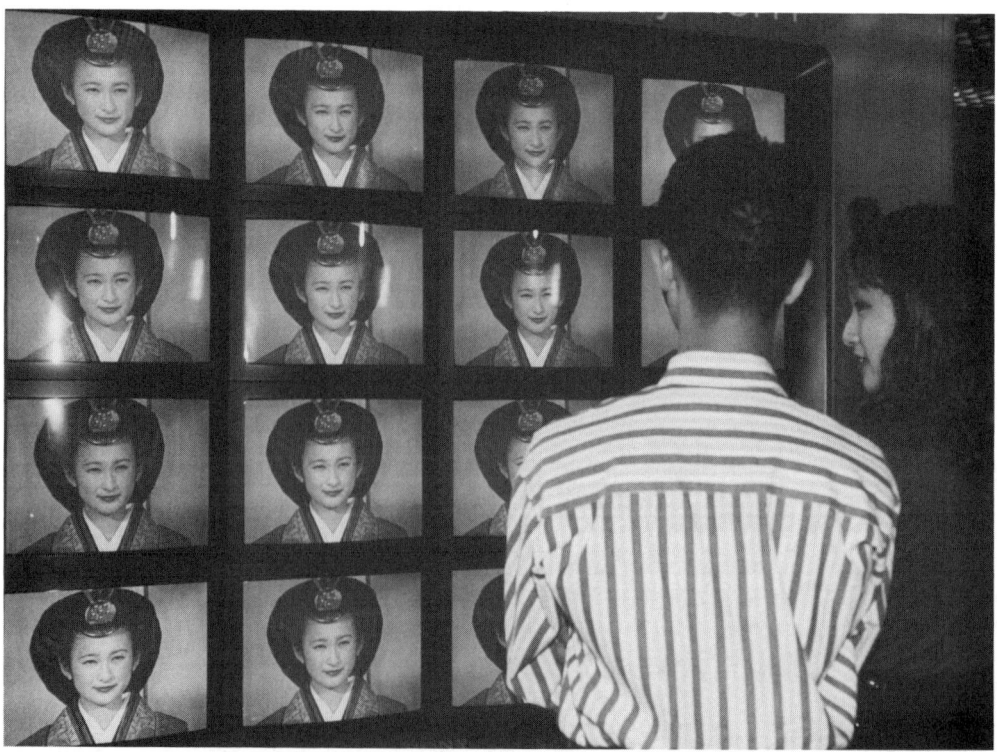

SELECTION 1

TUNE IN TO TV / **UNIT 8**

Watching television today is a very different experience from what it was forty years ago, as you will realize when you read **The Early Days and Beyond.**

BEFORE YOU READ

PREREADING DISCUSSION

1. Does everyone you know have a TV?
2. Do your parents or grandparents ever talk about the days before TV? What do they say?
3. How do you think your life would be different without TV?

BUILDING READING SKILLS

SKIMMING FOR MAIN IDEAS

Skim the following article one time quickly to find the answer to this question:

The purpose of "The Early Days and Beyond" is to _____.

a. give a history of television
b. explain how television works
c. predict television in the future
d. discuss why television is so bad

Now read the article again more carefully and do the exercises.

The Early Days and Beyond

1. The earliest experiments in television took place in the late 19th century. After the invention of the telephone in the 1870s, scientists began to wonder if pictures—like sound—could be transmitted through the air. However, it took many years of trial and error to get things right, because television cameras and receivers are complicated instruments.

2. The earliest television shows were often called telecasts or broadcasts. They were usually still pictures transmitted from one place to

another. However, in May 1928, General Electric's Schenectady station became the world's first regularly operating television station, simulcasting programs with GE's radio station for half an hour, three days a week. Television then merely added pictures to the sound that came from the radio.

3   In the early 1930s, telecasts were usually short and simple. Not many people had television sets to receive the pictures anyway! At the 1939 World's Fair in New York, television was a big hit. That year, Franklin D. Roosevelt became the first president to appear on television.

4   By the early 1940s, there were 23 television stations in the United States. But soon World War II brought a halt to the television industry. After the war, however, the craze to buy and watch TV really began.

5   By 1947, there were 170,000 TV sets in the United States. By the end of 1948, 250,000 people owned television sets. Two years later, that number had increased to over 4 million.

6   Only forty years ago, watching television was a totally different experience from what it is today. Then, the average family watched only black-and-white shows on a seven-inch screen. There were no remote control devices to change channels from the comfort of a sofa. Programs were aired only a few hours every evening.

7   However, the popularity of television pushed scientists to keep thinking up new ways to improve it. And they did. Color telecasts began in 1953. Larger screens, better reception, more—and more varied—shows, and remote-control devices are just some of the ways television has been improved.

8   Today, television is a communications system that links the far corners of the globe. And who knows what the future will bring.

TUNE IN TO TV / **UNIT 8**

BUILDING READING SKILLS

SCANNING FOR DETAILS

Scan the article and complete the paragraph with dates from the article.

The history of television began in the late _____ when scientists first started to experiment with the transmission of pictures through the air. It was not until years later, in _____, that the world's first real television station showed programs on a regular basis. At that time televisions broadcast the pictures, but the sound came from radios. Very few people owned television sets, and the shows in the _____ were short and simple. In _____, television made a big hit at the World's Fair. That same year, Franklin D. Roosevelt became the first American president to appear on TV. By _____ there were 170,000 TV sets in the United States. By the end of the next year, in _____, the number increased significantly, and 250,000 people owned TV sets. They were catching on quickly, and two years later, the number reached over 4 million. The popularity of television continued, and in _____, the first color telecasts began. Improvements in television have continued, and it seems certain that TV is here to stay.

FYi

The first country to have television was Great Britain (in 1936).

HOW WELL DID YOU READ?

Circle the letter of the choice that best completes the sentence.

1. Television really became popular _____.

   a. before World War II
   b. during the late nineteenth century
   c. after World War II

2. At first the telecasts were _____.

   a. long and complicated
   b. short and simple
   c. broadcast in color

(continued on the next page)

189

SELECTION 1

3. _____ was the first president of the United States to appear on TV.

   a. John Kennedy
   b. Richard Nixon
   c. Franklin D. Roosevelt

4. Only forty years ago, watching TV was _____ from what it is today.

   a. very different
   b. somewhat different
   c. almost the same

APPLICATION OF INFORMATION

Compare television forty years ago with TV today. Complete the chart with information from the article.

TV FORTY YEARS AGO	TV TODAY
Black and white	
	Larger screens

FIGURE IT OUT

VOCABULARY IN CONTEXT

Without using your dictionary, guess the meaning of the underlined words. Circle the letter of the word or phrase that is closest in meaning to the underlined word in each of the following sentences.

1. *After the invention of the telephone in the 1870s, scientists began to wonder if pictures—like sound—could be <u>transmitted</u> through the air.*

   a. bought
   b. sent
   c. increased

2. *However, it took many years of <u>trial and error</u> to get things right, because television cameras and receivers are complicated instruments.*

   a. trying different things and learning from mistakes
   b. going to court and talking to a judge
   c. returning damaged instruments

3. *At the 1939 World's Fair in New York, television was a <u>big hit</u>.*

   a. strong punch
   b. unpopular
   c. success

4. *By the early 1940s, there were 23 television stations in the United States. But soon World War II brought a <u>halt</u> to the television industry.*

   a. decision
   b. stop
   c. battle

5. *After the war, however, the <u>craze</u> to buy and watch TV really began.*

   a. popular fashion; fad
   b. technology
   c. suggestion

6. *Today, television is a communications system that <u>links</u> the far corners of the globe.*

   a. produces
   b. separates
   c. connects

FYI

The amount of TV people watch is determined by age and sex. Young children (26 hours per week), teenage boys (22 hours per week), and women over 55 (43 hours per week)[1].

[1] Louis Phillips, *TV Almanac*, (MacMillan, 1994).

SELECTION 2

Can you imagine a world without television? Some people think we would be better off without television in our lives. Others think it is one of the most important means of communication we have today. Read **Can You Imagine a World without It?** and see which side you are on.

BEFORE YOU READ

PREREADING ACTIVITY

Read each of these statements. Check the ones that are true for you.

_____ 1. Watching TV drains my energy.

_____ 2. I wouldn't mind not having a TV.

_____ 3. TV stimulates my mind.

_____ 4. I like to watch TV when I'm working or doing my homework.

_____ 5. TV commercials make me want to buy things I don't need.

_____ 6. I like to have the TV on for background noise.

_____ 7. Watching TV helps me relax.

_____ 8. I only turn the TV on to watch a specific program.

_____ 9. I have or would like to have a personal TV set.

• •

Can You Imagine a World without It?

1. Many people who are alive today know what it's like to live in a world without television. Television as we know it is only about forty years old. Yet it's so much a part of our lives that it seems as if it always existed.

2. Some people think that the years before television were a better time. They claim that families talked more and did more things together. More books were read. People used their imaginations more fully. People got more outdoor exercise.

3. But others disagree. They claim that television is a powerful educational tool. It informs us of what goes on in the world, from a

TUNE IN TO TV / **UNIT 8**

famine in Africa to a local fire. It entertains us. It helps shape our opinions about everything from politics to fashion. It helps us understand how people live, work, and struggle.

4   In 1961, Newton Minow, a government official, called prime-time schedules "a vast wasteland." Even though Minow said that over thirty years ago, many feel that it is still true today. Television is credited with being a great teacher. It is also blamed for the poor reading and writing skills of our population. Television gets praise for helping us understand the people of the world. But it has been accused of helping to destroy family life. Television keeps us informed about the political issues of the day. But it can also make us lazy by giving us only "news briefs" that are too short to tell the whole story.

5   Experts will probably continue to argue about television's value. But everyone agrees that it is one of the most significant inventions of the twentieth century. Even people who love television love to criticize it. As one writer put it, "Television influences everyone, and it pleases no one fully."

● ● ● ● ● ● ● ● ● ● ● ● ● ● ● ● ● ● ● ●

BUILDING VOCABULARY SKILLS

SYNONYMS AND ANTONYMS

Decide if the following pairs of words are synonyms or antonyms. If they are synonyms, circle S. If they are antonyms, circle A.

1. claim	state		S	A
2. inform	tell		S	A
3. significant	important		S	A
4. probably	likely		S	A
5. argue	agree		S	A
6. powerful	strong		S	A
7. issues	topics		S	A
8. lazy	active		S	A
9. whole	complete		S	A
10. criticize	blame		S	A

SELECTION 2

BUILDING READING SKILLS
UNDERSTANDING POINTS OF VIEW

Most people agree that TV has changed our lives. Some people feel the change has been good, but others disagree. They feel that the time before TV was probably better. How do you feel? Use ideas from the following list to complete one side of the chart. Add any other ideas that you can think of to support your choice.

1. TV is a powerful educational tool.
2. Families talked more and did more things together.
3. More books were read.
4. TV helps us understand how people live, work, and struggle.
5. We are entertained by TV.
6. People got more exercise.
7. TV informs us about what goes on in the world.
8. People used their imaginations more fully.

The years <u>before</u> TV were a better time because . . .	The years <u>since</u> TV have been a better time because . . .

FYI

Between the ages of two and sixty-five, the average American will watch 72,000 hours of TV, or a total of eight full years.

TUNE IN TO TV / **UNIT 8**

APPLICATION OF INFORMATION

Look at the following familiar photographs.

a. _____

b. _____

c. _____

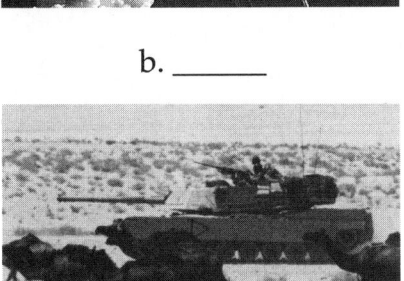

d. _____

e. _____

Now read the captions that go with the pictures. Match the captions with the appropriate picture by writing the number of the correct caption under each photo.

1. The assassination of President John Kennedy on November 22, 1963, shocked the world and plunged the United States into a state of deep mourning. Millions of people were glued to their TV sets watching the news of his death and funeral.

2. On July 20, 1969, 723 million people watched as Neil Armstrong and "Buzz" Aldrin became the first people to set foot on the moon. When they first landed the *Apollo 11* lunar module, Armstrong uttered the well-known statement, "That's one small step for man, one giant leap for mankind." While on the moon, they performed scientific experiments.

3. When Prince Charles of Great Britain and Lady Diana Spenser married on July 29, 1981, it was a spectacular affair. The TV audience included 700 million people in seventy-four countries.

4. By January of 1986, NASA had successfully completed fifty-five missions into space. However, on January 28, 1986, the space shuttle *Challenger* exploded shortly after it took off. Millions of TV viewers around the world watched in horror as the shuttle burned in space.

5. The Persian Gulf War in January of 1991 brought the realities of war into homes all around the world. Rocket launches and explosions in the sky over Baghdad were televised live and around the clock.

SELECTION 3

Henry Becton is the president and general manager of WGBH Educational Foundation. WGBH is part of the Public Broadcasting System (PBS). It is known for its high-quality educational and cultural television programs. Its programs reach approximately 34 million people per week, all over the United States. As president, Becton manages the 1,000 employees at WGBH and the $130 million budget.

In **Commercial-Free TV,** Henry Becton talks about public television: its purpose, its public, and how it gets its money and programming ideas.

BEFORE YOU READ

UNDERSTANDING VOCABULARY

The following interview is challenging. There may be some words you do not know. Discuss the meanings of the following words with your teacher and classmates before you read the interview.

promote	citizenship	stimulate	funding
origins	enrich	atmosphere	
humanities	experts	contributions	

Now read the interview one time and discuss it in small groups. If there are parts of it you do not understand, perhaps someone in your group can help you. Remember that you do not have to understand every word in the interview. Be satisfied with an understanding of the main ideas.

TUNE IN TO TV / **UNIT 8**

Commercial-Free TV

WGBH

What do you think is the purpose of public television?

1   I think the purpose of public TV is best expressed in our mission statement.[1] It says, "Our mission is to promote, through broadcasting or other means, the general education of the public by offering programs that inform, stimulate, and entertain, so that persons of all ages, origins, and beliefs may be encouraged, in an atmosphere of artistic freedom, to learn and appreciate the history, the sciences, the humanities, the fine arts, the practical arts, the music, the politics, the economics, and other significant aspects of the world they live in, and thereby to enrich and improve their lives."

How does public TV differ from commercial television?

2   Commercial television has become a way of selling products. It provides news and entertainment programs during some of its air time and sells the rest of its air time to advertisers. Programs that attract the most viewers are the most valuable to advertisers. On the other hand, public television has no advertising. Also, programs on public TV do not depend on popularity ratings to stay on the air. Public TV aims to reach smaller audiences. But we also want to give most of our viewers at least one program each week that they find valuable. In other words, public TV is here to serve the informational, cultural and educational, and citizenship needs of the public.

---

[1] **mission statement** A formal, written statement of the purpose of an organization.

SELECTION 3

Since your station doesn't get money from advertising, who pays for WGBH?

3   We get our money from a variety of sources. This funding comes from PBS and the Corporation for Public Broadcasting. We also get money from foundations,[2] federal and state governments, corporations, and most importantly from individual contributors.

Where do you get the ideas for programming?

4   There are lots of ideas everywhere. Many people have suggested an interesting concept for a documentary or "how-to" program. We get ideas from viewers, staff, producers, content experts, and funding sources. We judge the ideas in four ways. First, does it meet an important audience need? Second, is it likely to find funding? Third, will it attract an audience? And finally, can the producer carry out the project? Often, good ideas do not become programs because there isn't enough money for the project.

[2]**foundations** Organizations that give money to support projects they believe in.

HOW WELL DID YOU READ?

A. Read the following statements. If a statement is true, write *T* on the line. If it is false, write *F*.

_____ 1. WGBH aims to promote the general education of the public.

_____ 2. WGBH offers many different types of programs.

_____ 3. Both public and commercial television have commercials during their programs.

_____ 4. Public television serves smaller audiences than commercial television.

_____ 5. WGBH gets money from many different sources.

_____ 6. It is difficult for WGBH to get ideas for programs.

_____ 7. Public TV programs do not depend on popularity ratings.

TUNE IN TO TV / **UNIT 8**

B. Answer the questions on the lines provided.

1. What is the purpose of WGBH?

   _____

   _____

2. What are the main differences between public television and commercial television?

   _____

   _____

3. List four sources of funding for WGBH.

   _____

   _____

   _____

   _____

4. Where does WGBH get ideas for programs? List four sources.

   _____

   _____

   _____

   _____

5. How does WGBH judge ideas for programs? List four ways.

   _____

   _____

   _____

   _____

SELECTION 3

BUILDING VOCABULARY SKILLS
SUFFIXES

The suffix *-er* means someone who does something. For example, a *teacher* is someone who teaches and a *baker* is someone who bakes. The suffix *-or* also means *someone who*. For instance, a *sailor* is someone who sails boats.

A. Write a definition for each of the following words.

1. painter _____
2. actor _____
3. director _____
4. soccer player _____
5. inventor _____

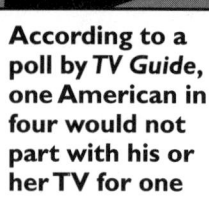

According to a poll by *TV Guide*, one American in four would not part with his or her TV for one million dollars.

B. Make a list of five other words that end in *-er* or *-or*. Share your list of words with your classmates.

1. _____
2. _____
3. _____
4. _____
5. _____

C. Look at the following examples of words taken from the interview you have just read. Write a definition for each one.

1. *But we also want to give most of our <u>viewers</u> at least one program each week that they find valuable.*

   _____

2. *We also get money from foundations, federal and state governments, corporations, and . . . individual <u>contributors.</u>*

   _____

TUNE IN TO TV / **UNIT 8**

3. *We get ideas from viewers, staff, producers, content experts, and funding sources.*

_____

4. *Programs that attract the most viewers are the most valuable to advertisers.*

_____

APPLICATION OF INFORMATION

CONDUCTING A SURVEY

Conducting a survey is a good way to collect information about people's habits and opinions. The following survey is about television viewing habits. Ask five people who are not in your class to answer the questions on this survey. Keep a record of their responses. Then bring the data you collected to class and combine it with the data your classmates collected.

1. On the average, how many hours of TV do you watch each day?

Less than one hour	One to three hours	Three to five hours	More than five hours

2. What kinds of shows do you like the best?

Comedies	Dramas	News	Talk Shows	Movies

(continued on the next page)

201

SELECTION 3

3. How do you usually get the news of the day?

By watching TV	By reading the newspaper	A combination of TV and newspapers

4. Do you turn on the TV to watch a specific show or do you turn it on to watch whatever is on?

Watch a specific show	Watch whatever is on

5. How much do TV commercials influence your purchasing decisions?

Very much	Somewhat	Not at all

Tabulate the information your whole class gathered from the survey. Make a chart to record your information.

[1] Source: Cartoon Network Europe.

Cartoons are popular with TV viewers everywhere. Here are the favorites in Europe:

- **Spain**
  The Jetsons
- **Norway**
  Yogi Bear
- **Sweden**
  Jonny Quest
- **Finland**
  Richie Rich
- **Holland**
  Captain Planet
- **U.K., Romania**
  The Flintstones
- **France, Poland**
  Bugs Bunny and Daffy Duck [1]

TYING IT ALL TOGETHER

TUNE IN TO TV / **UNIT 8**

DISCUSSION

1. Do you think that the news you see on TV is as accurate as the news you read in the paper? Why or why not?

2. Architect Frank Lloyd Wright has said, "Television is chewing gum for the eyes." What do you think he means? Do you think this is true?

3. Do you think that in the future the invention of the television will be considered as important as the invention of the printing press? Why or why not?

4. Do you think television has the power to make heroes? Explain your opinion. What is the difference between a hero and a celebrity?

5. Some people say that watching a sporting event on TV is better than being there in person. You get a close up look at the game's every play. You don't have to worry about the weather and you have experts to comment on the game as you watch. Do you prefer to see games on TV or in person? Why?

6. In what ways have cable channels such as MTV and CNN changed TV? What other changes can we expect in the future?

7. Discuss the effects of TV on each of the following:
   - advertising
   - politics
   - family life
   - violence

TV SCHEDULE

Make up your ideal TV schedule for one evening. Complete the chart by filling in the names of the channels (in the first column) and the names of the shows you would like to choose from (in the other columns). Share your TV guide with your classmates.

Channels	6:00	6:30	7:00	7:30	8:00	8:30	9:00	9:30	10:00	10:30

TYING IT ALL TOGETHER

JUST FOR FUN
WORD SEARCH

Find the seventeen words relating to television and circle them. The words may be horizontal, vertical, or diagonal. The first word has been found for you. Then check your answers in the Answer Key on page 211.

sports	drama	action
westerns	mysteries	situation comedies
soap opera	documentary	cartoons
cable	satellite	videotape
news	commercials	game shows
talk shows	PBS	

```
T O O R A N A I T A L K S H O W S A B S
D C O M M E R C I A L S A S D F G H J P
C A T W E O V W N V X O E H D R A M A O
W O F N E Z I P P Y S D D F W O C X M R
K O C N S S W X I C W X R Q U X X I Y T
C O M E T O T W D I S G A M E S H O W S
D O W N S W N E D O W V M Y I I E D E O
X O N P Z W N O R O P W A S X T C I W N
N M O N V G F S D N W C S T Q U B E X O
W O N C M C O W P B S O A E N A W O A W
W O V N W N X J K L S E R R T T W B T S
W C V I D E O T A P E D O I T I D O F S
F H W O N S X L W N W M C E X O D A O U
V A N O W N O O R S X W A S P N O H O K
D E C A D E N W O D N X O W J C C N A C
K W A C T I O N W S X O N J A O U P S D
D W B D O C N O P N W S X R O M M W A S
T W L D O X N O P Q N M E O W E E S T X
O Y E D W S C X K S O P A N O D N D E B
D W O N W O N B H G O I T Y O I T W L D
T Y S E N W O T O P N O P W S E A B L E
D O N S O L O W A L E F N I E S R W I A
A B C D E F G O I J K L M N O P Y O T E
W O V W K B S A P I E N C W O A E L E V
```

TUNE IN TO TV / **UNIT 8**

VOCABULARY REVIEW

WORK TOGETHER

In small groups, discuss the meaning of each of the following words from this unit. Write a definition or a synonym for each word. Try not to use your dictionary. Then, as a group, write a sentence for each word that shows you understand the meaning of the word. Share your sentences with the rest of the class.

1. promote _____
   _____

2. blame _____
   _____

3. significant _____
   _____

4. inform _____
   _____

5. experts _____
   _____

6. argue _____
   _____

7. lazy _____
   _____

8. origins _____
   _____

9. accuse _____
   _____

(continued on the next page)

TYING IT ALL TOGETHER

10. stimulate _____

_____

11. criticize _____

_____

12. enrich _____

_____

13. invention _____

_____

14. halt _____

_____

15. craze _____

_____

16. links _____

_____

SELF-TEST

Complete the sentences with words from the list.

promote	blame	lazy	significant
informed	argue	experts	origin
accused	stimulates	criticizes	enriches

1. Exercise is important to good health. It _____ the heart rate.

2. I think the accident was his fault. I _____ him.

3. Richard never gets any work done. He is so _____.

4. Pat finds something wrong with everything we do. She _____ us all the time.

5. Some people think there is too much violence on TV. They say it is a _____ amount.

6. She was told about the meeting. She was _____ where she should go for it and at what time.

7. We fought about it all weekend. I don't like it when we _____.

8. Some people feel that TV is valuable because it discusses meaningful and interesting issues. They think TV _____ their lives.

9. No one knows where the river begins. Its _____ is unknown.

10. The police thought Paul did it. They _____ him and arrested him.

11. Chronobiologists know a lot about the effects of time on the human body. They are _____ in that subject.

12. The sales department is working hard on the plans to sell the new product. They are figuring out how to _____ it.

READER'S JOURNAL

Think about the topics and ideas you have read about and discussed in this unit. Choose a topic and write about it for ten to twenty minutes. You may pick a topic from the following list or choose one of your own.

- your favorite show
- how TV is good or bad for children
- why you like or don't like to watch TV
- your thoughts on one of the questions from the Points to Ponder or Tying It All Together sections

TYING IT ALL TOGETHER

READER'S JOURNAL

Date: _____

ANSWER KEY

UNIT 2   JUST FOR FUN   page 51

ANIMAL GROUPS
1. colony of ants, 2. mob of kangaroos, 3. school of fish, 4. pride of lions, 5. swarm of bees, 6. troop of monkeys, 7. flock of sheep or geese, 8. pack of wolves, 9. bed of clams, 10. herd of elephants, 11. team of ducks or horses, 12. band of gorillas

ANIMAL EQUATIONS   page 52
1. TIE − E + FINGER − FIN = TIGER, 2. BABY − Y + MOON − M = BABOON, 3. BADGE + PEAR − PEA = BADGER, 4. CAN − N + MICE − ICE + ELBOW − BOW = CAMEL

UNIT 3   JUST FOR FUN   page 73

CROSSWORD PUZZLE

UNIT 4   page 90

BRAIN TEASERS
1. A quarter and a nickel. Only one of the coins is not a quarter. The other one *is* a quarter., 2. The parrot was deaf., 3. Survivors do not get buried., 4. When you meet, you are both the same distance from Boston., 5. They are triplets., 6. Twenty steps. The tide affects the ship as well as the ladder., 7. Twenty-seven. The spider will make one meter of progress every whole day., 8. a. Steve and Mary, b. Steve teaches the clarinet and the drums. Mary teaches the saxophone and the tuba., c. John, Carol, Tom, and David, d. John is learning the saxophone. Carol is learning the guitar. Tom is learning the drums. David is learning the tuba.

ANSWER KEY

UNIT 4 **JUST FOR FUN** page 97

PERSPECTIVE DRAWING
The following are some of the errors in perspective:

1. The tree and the house in the lower-right corner do not make sense in relation to the bridge.
2. The cat is too big.
3. There is water on only one side of the bridge.
4. There is no one driving the horse and cart.
5. The woman looks as though she is sitting in the tree.
6. The boat's anchor is not in the water in front of the boat.
7. The bird's feet are holding the swing.
8. The boat's sails are blowing in the opposite direction from the flag.
9. The fishing line goes into the well, not into the water behind the boat.

ANSWER KEY

UNIT 5   **JUST FOR FUN**   page 124

WEATHER FOLKLORE

1. True. Beekeepers have observed that bees lose their navigational systems when the weather is bad. Therefore, they stay close to their hives., 2. True. They are very accurate. Count their chirps for fourteen seconds. Then add forty and you will know the Fahrenheit temperature of the cricket's location., 3. False. People only wish that this were true., 4. False. Cows lie down when they are tired., 5. False. It would be nice if nature were so predictable and balanced, but it isn't., 6. True. Birds adjust their flight patterns to fly where the air pressure is the highest. When the barometric air pressure is high (good weather), they fly high. When the barometric pressure is low (bad weather) they fly low., 7. False. Nature is not so predictable., 8. True. Humidity causes them to close., 9. False. It means that they have eaten well and lived in good conditions., 10. True. Birds generally roost when air pressure is low., 11. False. Squirrels always gather as many nuts as they can. In some years there are more nuts available than in other years., 12. Often, but not always, true.

UNIT 6   **JUST FOR FUN**   page 149

LAST LETTER FIRST

1. salad, 2. dessert, 3. teriyaki, 4. ice cream, 5. meat, 6. tea, 7. avocado, 8. orange, 9. eggs, 10. spaghetti

UNIT 8   **JUST FOR FUN**   page 204

WORD SEARCH

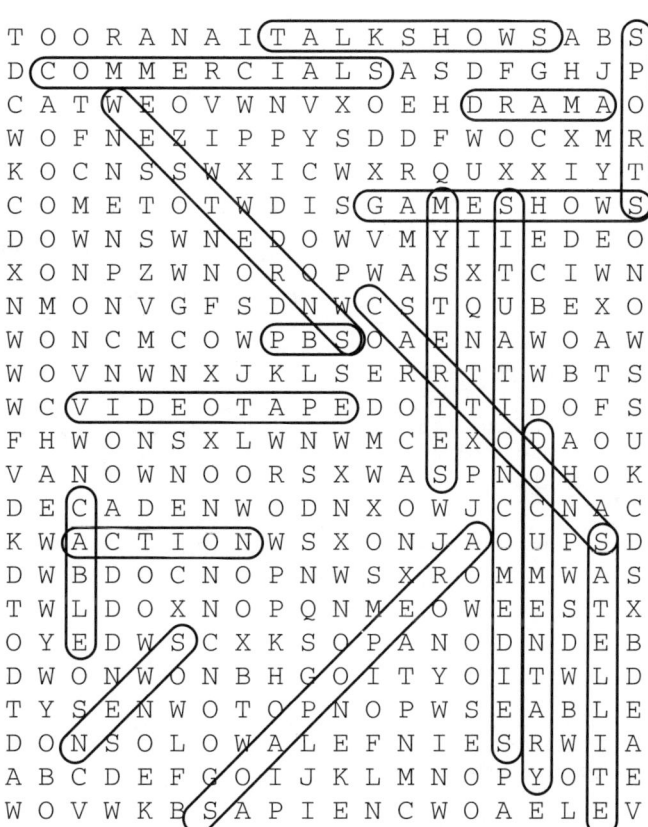

TEXT CREDITS

Grateful acknowledgment is given to the following publishing companies and individuals for permission to print, reprint, or adapt materials for which they own copyrights:

UNIT 1—Travel Talk

The Company of the Sea. Interview printed with the permission of Eralp Akkoyunlu.

Flying High, but Feeling Low. SOURCES: *Overcoming Jet Lag* by Dr. Charles Ehret and Lynne Waller Scanlon, Berkley Books, New York, 1983; "Jet Lag's New Pill," *Conde Nast Traveler,* April 1994.

UNIT 2—Attitudes About Animals

All for the Love of Fritz. Interview printed with the permission of Doris Davis.

Anti-Fur Groups Renew Fur Debate. Reprinted with the permission of NEWS FOR YOU (Syracuse, New York), from the March 23, 1994 issue.

Animal Equations. From *Perplexing Puzzles and Tantalizing Teasers* by Martin Gardner. Reprinted with the permission of Dover Publications, Inc.

UNIT 3—Facing Challenges

86-Year-Old Man in Marathon for 63rd Time. SOURCE: Adapted from "Ageless Kelley, Adoring Fans Have a Grand Old Time Together" by Bob Monahan, *The Boston Globe,* April 19, 1994.

Disabled People Find Challenge on the Slopes. Reprinted with the permission of NEWS FOR YOU (Syracuse, New York), from the March 23, 1994 issue.

Sounds of Bali. Interview printed with the permission of Desak Made Suarti Laksmi.

Dreams. From *The Dream Keeper and Other Poems* by Langston Hughes. Copyright 1932 by Alfred A. Knopf Inc. and renewed 1960 by Langston Hughes. Reprinted by permission of the publisher.

UNIT 4—Brainpower

Are You Right-Brained or Left-Brained? Reprinted courtesy of TEEN Magazine, November 1993 issue.

Albert Einstein: The Man and the Legends about Him. The following adaptation is reprinted with the permission of PROVOKING THOUGHTS (Austin, Minnesota), from the May–June 1991 issue.

How Good Is Your Memory? Interview printed with the permission of Diane Englund.

UNIT 5—Climate Control

Quiz. From the dust cover of *Seasons of the Mind* by Dr. Norman Rosenthal, Bantam, 1989. Reprinted with the permission of the author.

Winter Blues, Summer Blahs. SOURCES: *Seasons of the Mind* by Dr. Norman Rosenthal, Bantam, 1989; "Sizing up Sadness According to Latitude" by B. Bower, *Science News,* Vol. 136, page 198; "Cold Weather Blues," *Ladies Home Journal,* January 1989, page 92.

Climate: A Powerful Force. SOURCES: *Ice or Fire? Surviving Climatic Changes* by D.S. Halacy Jr., Harper and Row, New York, 1978; *The Challenge of Climate: Man and His Environment* by Robert Silverberg, Meredith Press, New York, 1969; "Climate" by John A. Harrington Jr., *World Book Encyclopedia,* Vol. 4, pages 676–680. World Book, Inc., A. Scott Fetzre Co., 1989; "Climate and the Rise of Man" by William F. Allman with Betsy Wagner, *U.S. News and World Report,* June 8, 1992, pages 60–67.

What's the Weather? Interview printed with the permission of David Cook.

UNIT 6—Food for Thought

Quiz. SOURCE: Adapted from "Your Nutritional Snapshot," *Eat Right the E.A.S.Y. Way* by Joan Salge Blake, M.S., R.D., Prentice Hall Press, New York, 1991, page 9.

Finding the Recipe for Success. Interview printed with the permission of Elisabeth Rozin, author of *The Flavor-Principle Cookbook, Ethnic Cuisine, Blue Corn and Chocolate,* and *The Primal Cheeseburger.*

Genetically Altered Tomato Approved. Reprinted with the permission of NEWS FOR YOU (Syracuse, New York), from the June 8, 1994 issue.

Red Hot, or Not? Adapted from "Chile Peppers," from the September 1994 issue of 3-2-1 CONTACT Magazine. Copyright 1994 Children's Television Workshop, New York. All rights reserved.

UNIT 7—Companies with a Conscience

Profits with Principles. SOURCES: "Anita Roddick" by Pope Brock, *People Magazine,* May 10, 1993, pages 101–106; "The Body Shop International" Harvard Business School Case # 9-392-032. Harvard Business School, Boston, MA, 02163, pages 1–9.

The Scoop on Ben & Jerry's. Interview printed with the permission of Mitch Curren, Coordinator of Public Relations for Ben & Jerry's.

Warm and Fuzzy Soda Bottles. From a letter written by Lu Setnika, Public Affairs Director for Patagonia. Reprinted with the permission of Lu Setnika.

UNIT 8—Tune in to TV

The Early Days and Beyond and **Can You Imagine a World without It?** Adapted from "Television" by Michael Adams, KIDS DISCOVER, March 1992 issue. Reprinted with the permission of KIDS DISCOVER.

Commercial-Free TV. Interview printed with the permission of Henry Becton, President and General Manager of WGBH Educational Foundation.